126W

13⁰⁰

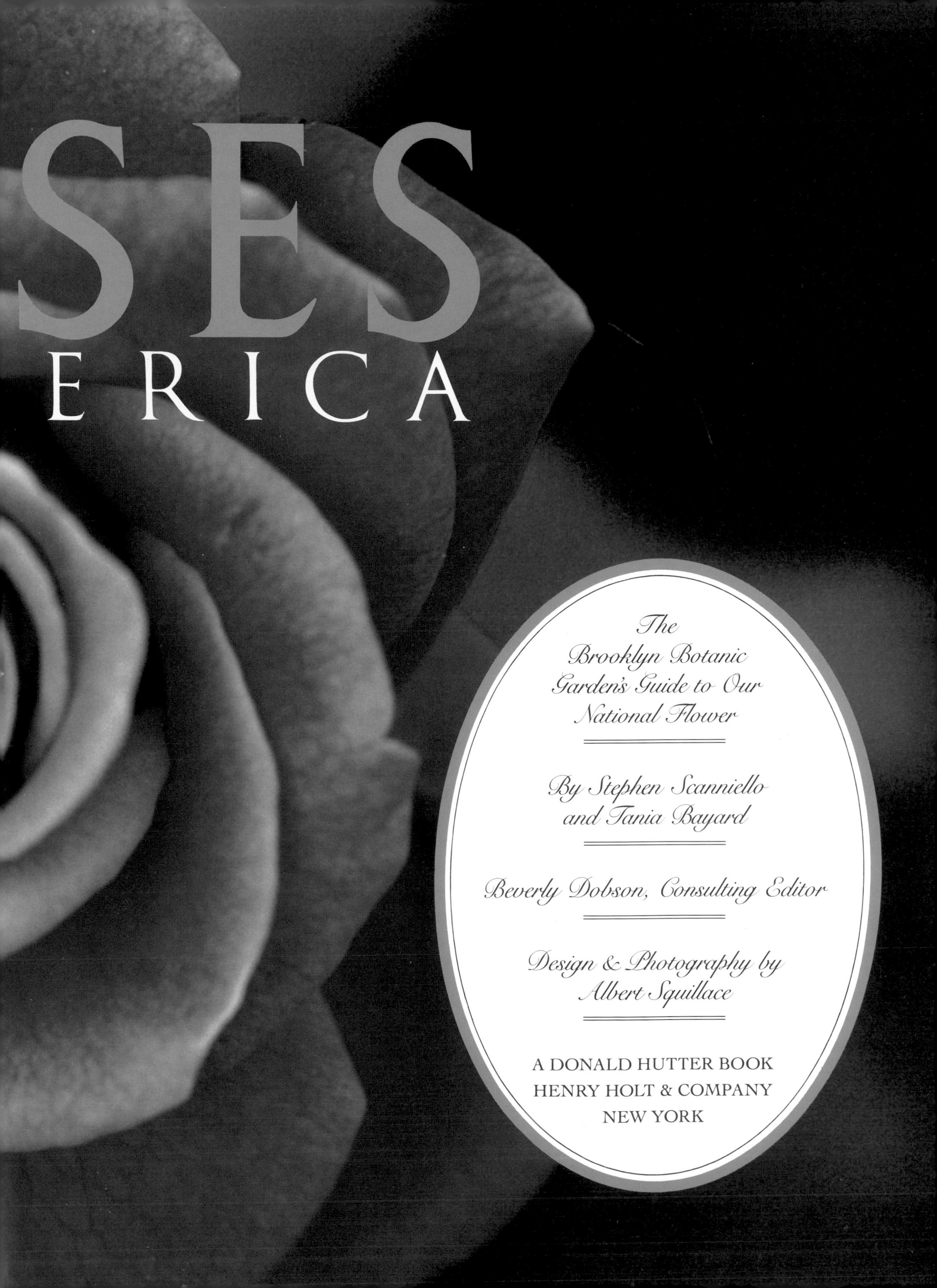

# SES
# ERICA

The
Brooklyn Botanic
Garden's Guide to Our
National Flower

―――――

By Stephen Scanniello
and Tania Bayard

―――――

Beverly Dobson, Consulting Editor

―――――

Design & Photography by
Albert Squillace

A DONALD HUTTER BOOK
HENRY HOLT & COMPANY
NEW YORK

Published by Henry Holt and Company, Inc.,
115 West 18th Street, New York, New York 10011.
Published in Canada by Fitzhenry & Whiteside Limited,
195 Allstate Parkway, Markham, Ontario L3R 4TR.

### Library of Congress Cataloging-in-Publication Data

Scanniello, Stephen,
    Roses of America : the Brooklyn Botanic Garden's guide to our
national flower / Stephen Scanniello and Tania Bayard : Beverly
Dobson, consulting editor : photography by Albert Squillace.
    — 1st ed.
        p.  cm.
    "A Donald Hutter book,"
    Includes bibliographical references and index.
    ISBN 0-8050-1241-9
    1. Roses—United States.   2. Roses.   3. Rose culture—United
States.   4. Rose culture.   5. Rose gardens—United States.
    I. Bayard, Tania.   II. Brooklyn Botanic Garden.   III. Title.
SB411.S32   1990                                              90-4779
635.9'33372'0973—dc20                                          CIP

Henry Holt books are available at special discounts
for bulk purchases for sales promotions, premiums,
fund-raising, or educational use. Special editions or book
excerpts can also be created to specification.
For details contact:
Special Sales Director
Henry Holt and Company, Inc.
115 West 18th Street
New York, New York 10011

**First Edition**

Produced and prepared by Sammis Publishing Corp.
and Layla Productions, Inc.

Art Director: ALBERT SQUILLACE
Project Director: BARBARA PESCH
Project Editor: LORI STEIN
Art Associate: CHANI YAMMER

10 9 8 7 6 5 4 3 2 1

## Acknowledgments

The authors wish to thank the many people who have given
of their time and expertise to help in the creation of this book:
Donald Moore, Elizabeth Scholtz, Elvin McDonald,
Janet Marinelli, Edmond O. Moulin, Brenda Weisman, Dr. Kerry Barringer and
Deborah Krupczak at the Brooklyn Botanic Garden; Katherine Powis
at the Horitcultural Society of New York; Lothian Lynas and
Bernadette Callery at the New York Botanical Garden; Kathy Grosfils
at the Colonial Williamsburg Society; Paige Savery at the Connecticut
Historical Society; Liz Christy at the Bowery Houston Community Garden.
Mike Shoup at the Antique Rose Emporium. Jane Fire at the Museum
of American Folk Art; The All-America Rose Selections; The American Rose Society;
also Peter Beales, Virginia Hopper, Jeannie Fernsworth, Susan Littlefield, Peter Bertrand,
Mrs. Esther Jasik, Dr. and Mrs. Thomas Alderson, Mr. and Mrs. William Morton,'
Mr. and Mrs. David Malcolm, Mr. and Mrs. Vincent Cassanetti,
Mrs. John J. McCloy II, Mr. and Mrs. Patrick Markham,
Mr. and Mrs. Mark and Nancy K. Farran, K. Mose Fadem, Dr. Peter Nelson,
Teddie Slater, Jay Hyams, Leslie Garisto, Chani Yammer, Anne Miller,
David Prior, Ed Fleischer, Laurie Conlin, John Sammis, and
the late Donald Hutter. Special thanks to Robert M. Cammarota,
Dana Twining, photographer and art director Albert Squillace,
Brooklyn Botanic Garden Director of Publications
Barbara Pesch, Vice-President of Science Dr. Steven K-M. Tim, Beverly and
Stuart Dobson, and our indefatigable editor, Lori Stein.

## Photography Credits:

All photographs are by Albert Squillace with
the following exceptions:
Abby Aldrich Rockefeller Folk Art Center, Williamsburg, Virginia: p. 13
All-America Rose Selections: p. 121
Colonial Williamsburgh Foundation, Photograph by Laura Viancour: p. 15 top
Connecticut Historical Society, Hartford Connecticut: p. 21
Christine Douglas: p.65
K. Mose Fadem: p. 15 bottom left
Heritage Rose Foundation: p. 79 top left
Margaret Falk: pp. 45 top left, 64 top left
Museum of American Folk Art: p. 14 top right.
New York Botanical Garden: p.16 top left, bottom left
Mike Shoup: p. 154
Stephen Scanniello: pp. 14 top left, 40 top right; 41; 45 bottom left,
48 bottom right; 61, 63 bottom left, 66 top left, 69 top right;
73 bottom left; 89 top left and right; 114 top; 117; 138 right.
William Paca Garden: pp. 14 bottom, 15 bottom right
United States Botanical Garden: p. 166
Photographs on pages 192-211 were submitted by the gardens shown.

Typesetting by Midatlantic Photocomposition

Front jacket illustration: 'World Peace'
Back jacket illustration: The Cranford Rose Garden

To all the volunteers, past and present,
and especially to my mother and father, who have
helped in the Cranford Rose Garden

STEPHEN SCANNIELLO

To the memory of my parents, who inspired me
with their beautiful gardens and their love of nature.

TANIA BAYARD

# Contents

# Preface

A Brooklyn Botanic Garden president must get used to the idea that the world regards him or her as considerably less important than the gardeners.

This was brought home to me with force in my first year at the Garden by titled visitors from Scotland—an Earl and His lady. They were polite to me, but plainly they were here to consult with the arborist. It seems there are trees in our collection that might bring new autumn color to the castle grounds, which in turn might bring more paying visitors.

Peter Malins, then the rosarian, was the author of a popular book on his subject. Frank Okamura, the bonsai master, was awarded a medal by the Emperor of Japan. Jacqueline Fazio, curator of the Local Flora Section, was featured in articles about wildflowers. Daniel Ryniec became president of the International Lilac Society and Ira Walker was elected to the board of the American Conifer Society.

And so it comes as no surprise that Stephen Scanniello, the second great rosarian I have known at the Garden, has now co-authored a great book on roses. What else? After lecture tours throughout North America, television appearances, research forays through Europe, what else would he do but a book?

All of the people associated with the Garden—his fellow gardeners, the scientists, the teachers, and perhaps most of all the numberless volunteers who work in the rose garden—are of course proud of what Steve and co-author Tania Bayard have accomplished here.

We know the information is authoritative. We know the book is a valuable addition to any gardener's library. And we know that with this new boost to his spreading fame, there will be even more prominent visitors asking for Mr. Scanniello, the rosarian. All I can ask is that some of them make some effort to be kind to the Garden's president, Judith Zuk.

DONALD MOORE
*President of the Brooklyn Botanic Garden, 1980–1990.*

In a world where technology has facilitated duplication of the written word, the need to be selective about what one publishes becomes a decided responsibility. The decision for this book reflects this very standpoint; it fills a gap in the literature already available on the subject . . . it is especially for America and Americans.

The earliest influences on rose-growing in America were from European immigrants who included news about Asian species. America was soon part of the international rose-growing and hybridizing fraternity but literature on these as garden plants continued to be strongly influenced by the European experience.

Over the past 60 years, information about the growing and selection of roses in America has been accumulated by the Brooklyn Botanic Garden, from the original architect, gardeners, volunteers and curators associated with the Cranford Rose Garden. Their wide-ranging quest for rose-growing know-how resulted in the accumulation of growing experiences from around the country. I am pleased that these experiences and those gleaned from tending the over 5,000 rose bushes in Brooklyn are now presented with American conditions specifically in mind.

STEPHEN K-M. TIM
*Vice-President, Science and Publications*

# 1 The Rose in America

# *The Rose in America*

*Yea, in May you shall see the Woods and Fields so
curiously bedecke with Roses . . . that you may behold
Nature contending with Art, and striving to equal, if not
excel many Gardens in England.*

DANIEL DENTON,            A Brief Description of New-York, 1670

n 1986, Congress proclaimed the rose the national flower of the United States. Official recognition was unnecessary, however; the rose had been America's favorite flower from the days when the earliest settlers rejoiced to find delightful native wild roses blooming in the strange new land. Today roses have a special place in our gardens, our homes, and all our celebrations and important events, from weddings and holidays to the Rose Bowl.

One of the first roses the settlers must have noticed was *Rosa virginiana*, which ranges over a large part of eastern North America. The British herbalist John Parkinson described this rose with flesh-pink flowers and small, shining leaves, in his *Theatrum Botanicum* (*Theatre of Plants*) in 1640. Native American roses were among the many exotic discoveries from the New World that fascinated the Europeans. Plants of *R. virginiana* were shipped from Virginia to England in 1724, making it one of the earliest North American roses known to have been cultivated in Europe. *Rosa palustris*, the Swamp Rose, was another native American rose sent abroad in the

eighteenth century; an enterprising Philadelphia nurseryman, William Young, listed it under other names in his 1783 catalogue of plants for export to France. Thomas Jefferson sent "seeds of wild roses of every kind, a half bushel of each," to a friend in France in 1803.

The colonists brought other roses from home — the albas, damasks, centifolias, gallicas, and sweetbriers that had been cultivated in Europe since antiquity for their beauty, fragrance, and medicinal properties. Early American housewives, relying on practical knowledge going back thousands of years, carried seeds and cuttings of these roses to their new homes and planted them for use in medications, cooking, sachets, deodorants, and handwashing waters. The importance of roses went far beyond mere usefulness, however. Like the British garden writer Thomas Hyll, who wrote in 1577, "Of all the Flowers in the Garden, [the Rose] is the chief for beauty and sweetness," early Americans grew roses simply because they were lovely.

At first, the garden roses in America were limited to the few types that had been grown in Europe since ancient times. But during the late

*Above: Rosa carolina, a native North American rose. Opposite: Portrait of Deborah Glen, ca. 1739.
Artist unknown. Albany, New York area. Abby Aldrich Rockefeller Folk Art Center, Williamsburg, Virginia.*

*Top left:* The first settlers in America found several species of wild roses including *Rosa virginiana*, whose hips are pictured above. *Top right:* Images of roses often appeared in early American art, such as this detail of a stencil painting, ca. 1835. *Above:* the rose parterre at the William Paca Garden, Annapolis, Maryland.

Restored gardens. *Top:* The Cherokee Rose, growing in the restored gardens of Colonial Williamsburg in Virginia. *Above:* The 1897 cook's house with its rose arbor at the recently restored Cooper-Molera garden on the Monterey Peninsula, California. *Right: R. foetida* at the William Paca Garden, built ca. 1770.

*15*

*Top:* Pages from the 1822 edition of the catalog from Prince's, the first major nursery. *Above left:* Revolutionary War currency with a rose leaf motif. *Above right:* Advertisement for Conard & Pyle's *How to Grow Roses,* from an early *American Rose Annual.* *Left:* Illustration by Redoute of 'Champney's Pink Cluster', which led to a new class, the Noisettes. *Right:* An early illustrated rose catalog, from The Storrs and Harrison Company catalog for fall, 1888.

eighteenth and early nineteenth centuries, when newly discovered everblooming roses from the Far East were brought to the West and crossed with European roses, there was an explosive increase in varieties. Scores of new roses were exported to America.

Books and catalogues put out by nurserymen are a valuable source of information on the numbers and kinds of roses available in early America. In 1790, Prince's, the first major American nursery (founded in 1737 on Long Island by Robert Prince), listed only twelve varieties in its catalogue: moss, musk, centifolia, gallica, cinnamon, yellow, monthly (as the newly discovered repeating China roses were called), thornless, American wild roses, two types of damask, and primroses (the last-named probably not roses at all). When William Robert Prince, the great grandson of the founder, published the *Prince Manual of Roses* in 1846, he listed 1,630 varieties, an indication of how large the demand for the new roses, known in the trade as hardy perpetual roses, had become.

By 1844, roses were so important to the business of Robert Buist, a Scottish nurseryman in Philadelphia, that he published *The Rose Manual*, the first book in America devoted entirely to roses. Buist, who claimed he had the largest collection of roses in the country, was one of a number of horticulturists who encouraged ladies to grow their own plants; roses were among those especially recommended because they could be successfully cultivated indoors in containers.

Buist was a prominent exhibitor of roses in American flower shows. At the first of these shows, sponsored in 1829 by the Pennsylvania Horticultural Society, roses were the second most important class. In 1835, there were 132 varieties of roses in one exhibition alone at the Massachusetts Horticultural Society Flower Show, and by the 1870s an annual show devoted solely to roses had been established by that society.

Not all of the hundreds of roses brought to this country in the nineteenth century fared well, however. In 1882, H. B. Ellwanger published *The Rose*, a book that soon set the standard for rose classification. Ellwanger, proprietor of the Mount Hope Nursery in Rochester, New York,

described and evaluated nearly a thousand varieties of roses in his book, but he complained that many of them were European imports unsuitable for cultivation in America. Not one to mince words, he evaluated some of the roses on his list as "not worth growing," "not very promising," "worthless," and in one case, "a humbug." Of the seventy breeders of roses he listed as the best in the world, only seven were Americans, and he felt that this country needed more rose hybridizers of its own. Ellwanger himself attempted to develop roses that would grow well in the United States, using native wild roses as the stock.

Americans in the early part of the nineteenth century had made some significant contributions to the creation of new roses, beginning around 1811 when John Champneys in Charleston, South Carolina, raised 'Champneys' Pink Cluster,' a rose that led to a new class, the Noisettes. In the 1830s and 1840s, Samuel and John Feast in Baltimore, Maryland, experimented with the native American climber, *Rosa setigera*, the Prairie Rose, and produced a number of hardy climbers that were useful for American gardens because they could withstand severe winters. There were several other important rose breeders in this country in the early nineteenth century, but it was only after the introduction of rugged wild roses from Asia that Americans moved to the forefront of rose hybridizing.

In the late nineteenth century, plants of *Rosa wichuraiana*, a wild rose discovered in Japan, were sent from a nursery in Berlin to the Arnold Arboretum in Massachusetts, where botanists were assembling a collection of hardy plants from all the temperate regions of the world. Hybridizers in America were intrigued with this vigorous rose (called the Memorial Rose because people used it for grave plantings), and they began to experiment with it, as well as with *Rosa rugosa* and *Rosa multiflora*, other sturdy Asiatic wild roses. Many American nurserymen, realizing that these Asiatic species could flourish in the severe climates and varying soils of the United States, developed successful climbers and shrubs by crossing them with existing cultivated varieties.

In response to the increasing interest in roses in this country, the American Rose Society

Garden publications proliferated in America from the early 1800s on.
*Top:* Two editions of *The Rose*, by H. B. Ellwanger. *Above:* Jackson &
Perkins catalog (Fall, 1922).

*Top:* How-to article from *How to Grow Roses* by Horace McFarland. *Center left: Dreer's Garden Book* (1928). *Center right: Roses,* by Bobbink & Atkins, 1922. *Above:* Several catalogs from the 1940s. *Above right:* J. Horace McFarland's well-known volume, *The Rose in America,* 1923.

## J. Horace McFarland
## (1859 - 1948)

During its early years, the American Rose Society was essentially a small association of commercial nurserymen. The man who transformed it into a dynamic organization of dedicated amateur as well as professional rose growers was J. Horace McFarland, president of the society from 1930–1932, who published the first *American Rose Annual* in 1916 and served as editor of the prestigious yearbook for nearly thirty years.

McFarland was a man of unlimited interests and the energy with which to pursue them. A printer by trade—he owned and operated the Mount Pleasant Press in Harrisburg, Pennsylvania—he was also a horticulturist and an accomplished photographer who developed the art of color photography in this country. He combined all these talents by specializing in the printing of colored garden catalogues. Breeze Hill, his garden in Harrisburg, became famous because he used photographs of his own plants as the illustrations in these publications.

McFarland, a largely self-educated man who was proud of the honorary degree of Doctor of Humane Letters he received from Dickinson College in 1924, was an avid conservationist who worked for the establishment and preservation of America's national parks and helped to save Niagara Falls from commercial exploitation. At home he was a serious gardener, and roses were his special love. Of the numerous books he wrote on gardening, four were about roses, and he was tireless in his efforts to realize the ARS motto: "A rose for every home, a bush for every garden." His efforts on behalf of the rose went far beyond his work for the society, however. As head of the American Civic Association, which he founded in 1904, he organized a "Crusade Against Ugliness," a campaign in which the rose was foremost among the plants he recommended for the beautification of American cities and towns. He saw uses for roses everywhere—along highways and railroad embankments, in parks and public gardens, on institutional grounds, and above all in home gardens. He even introduced his favorite flower to penal institutions, helping a prisoner establish a rose garden at Sing Sing, and encouraging a rose-growing parolee at San Quentin. When the government of the United States was deciding what coronation gift to send to Emperor Haile Selassie of Ethiopia in 1930, Horace McFarland made sure it was roses—437 bushes of 62 varieties of American origin, to be planted in the royal gardens in Addis Ababa.

Breeze Hill, J. Horace McFarland's home in Harrisburg, Pennsylvania.

(ARS) was founded in 1899. The ARS, which today has about twenty thousand members and many chapters and affiliated societies, has been very instrumental in promoting roses and disseminating knowledge about them in the United States. In the pages of its yearbook, the *American Rose Annual*, first published in 1916, we can follow the progress of the early twentieth-century hybridizers who were attempting to provide, in the words of the ARS motto, "a rose for every home, a bush for every garden"—a difficult task in a country with such disparate climates and growing conditions.

By 1930, Americans had introduced hundreds of successful new varieties of roses. In that year, Congress passed the Plant Patent Act, providing much-needed protection for hybridizers. Up until that time, any plant that went on the market became common property, and the breeder lost all rights to it. The Plant Patent Act granted to anyone who discovered or hybridized a

Elizabeth Park, Hartford, Connecticut, the first municipal rose garden in America, designed by Theodore Worth and opened in 1904. By 1930 there were important municipal rose gardens in at least thirty states.

new plant the exclusive right to determine for seventeen years who would propagate and sell it. The first plant in the world to be patented under this law was an American climbing rose, 'New Dawn', introduced by Henry Dreer in 1930.

Great municipal rose gardens, where the ever-increasing number of roses could be displayed, were developed in the United States early in this century. The first of these was in Elizabeth Park, Hartford, Connecticut, designed and planted in 1904 by Theodore Worth, who later established a similar rose garden in Lyndale Park, Minneapolis, Minnesota. In 1915, the National Rose Garden in Washington, D.C., which was presented to the U. S. government by the American Rose Society, was dedicated. By 1930, there were important municipal rose gardens in at least thirty states and special sections devoted to roses in many botanical gardens; one of these was the great collection in the Cranford Rose Garden at the Brooklyn Botanic Garden.

Inspired by these gardens, more Americans than ever were growing roses at home, and the All-America Rose Selections (AARS) was founded in 1938 to help them choose the best varieties. Growers from all over the world submit new roses for testing in twenty-one AARS trial gardens at universities and firms around the country, and over a period of two years, experienced judges rate these roses for their disease resistance, hardiness, flowers, form, and ability to grow in the differing climates of the United States. The AARS award winners chosen at the end of the trial period comprise only about four percent of all the roses tested; naturally, sales of these varieties are greatly enhanced by the distinction. There are also 132 AARS-accredited public gardens nationwide where people can observe the award winners a year before they go on the market and evaluate their performance in that particular region of the country. The Cranford Rose Garden is one of these gardens.

*21*

2 The Cranford

Rose Garden

## 2

# The Cranford Rose Garden

n 1927, Walter V. Cranford, a construction engineer whose firm was responsible for several sections of Brooklyn's subway systems, picked up a copy of the Brooklyn Botanic Garden annual report and noticed that a rose garden was planned — at an estimated cost of $10,000. Like so many others throughout history, Cranford was enchanted by the idea of a garden of roses, and he presented the Brooklyn Botanic Garden with the money. Work began immediately on what was to become one of the most important rose collections in the United States.

The Cranford Rose Garden was designed by Harold Caparn, consulting landscape architect for the Brooklyn Botanic Garden, and Montague Free, the Garden's horticulturist. Caparn had drawn up the plans for the garden several years earlier, and construction began on June 14, 1927, four days after Cranford's check was received. The excavations uncovered an old cobblestone road, two large roadside drains, and enormous glacial rocks that had to be broken up before they could be carted away. At least twenty-eight two-horse loads of stone were removed, at the cost of four worn-out plowshares and two sets of broken harnesses. When Cranford visited the garden in October 1927, he saw that $10,000 would not cover the cost of all the work, and he donated an additional $5,000. In the fall of 1927, one thousand rosebushes were planted. The garden opened to the public in June 1928, and later that year the number of plants was increased to three thousand — 650 different species and varieties in all.

Summer visitors who approach the Cranford Rose Garden from The Overlook, the hill that rises above it to the north, look out over an expanse of lawns and trees in the center of which a myriad of roses sparkle like jewels in a green setting. Covering a rectangular area of about one acre, the formally arranged garden is separated from its surroundings by white wooden trellises and a white latticework pavilion on a mound at the south end: from this mound one can see the entire collection. A triangular area containing additional roses extends south beyond the pavilion. Originally, a Doric pergola completed the enclosure on the north, but this was not replaced after it blew over in a storm in 1938;

View of the Cranford Rose Garden facing south.

BROOKLYN BOTANIC GARDEN

FOURTEENTH ANNUAL
### SPRING INSPECTION
BY TRUSTEES, WOMAN'S AUXILIARY
MEMBERS, AND INVITED GUESTS
TUESDAY, MAY 8th, 1928
3:30—6:00 P. M.

### PROGRAM
The tour of inspection will start from the Laboratory Building promptly at 3:30 o'clock.

Guests, accompanied by young ladies as guides, will be conducted in groups of convenient size. Members of the Garden Staff will be stationed at convenient points to give explanations and answer questions.

### ITINERARY
1. JAPANESE GARDEN. Improvements by Japanese workmen are now in progress, under the general supervision of Miss Mary Averill, Honorary Curator of Japanese Gardening and Floral Art.

Just north of this Garden about 45 *Flowering Crabs* were planted this spring to serve as a background for a further extension of the Iris collection.

2. CHERRY WALK. It is expected that the two rows of flowering cherries along this walk will be in flower on the day of the inspection.

3. THE NEW ROSE GARDEN

This garden is the gift of Mr. and Mrs. Walter V. Cranford, of Greenwich, Conn.
*View from the Museum Embankment.*

In the foreground the *North Pergola.*

Beyond, the 15 *beds* in three rows of five beds each, and the *border planting* on each side.

The garden during its construction in 1927, from sketch to preparation of soil to completion and the first annual rose day. *Opposite bottom left:* Program for opening of the rose garden. *Right:* From left to right, Dr. Stuart Gager, Mrs. Walter V. Cranford, Mr. Walter V. Cranford, Miss Hilda Loines, Mr. Edward C. Blum, Mrs. Edward C. Blum, Dr. J.H. Nicolas, Mr. Harold A. Caparn, Mr. Montague Free.

*Above:* People entering pavilion on an early rose day. *Right:* 'Dr. Van Fleet' growing on a pavilion window in the early years of the Cranford garden. This rose still grows here today, over sixty years later. *Top and opposite:* Views of the pavilion, in the 1920s and today.

now an uninterrupted display of roses spreads up the hill to The Overlook.

Caparn was an advocate of roses that were out of favor in the 1920s: the wild roses and the classes of roses that had been known prior to the creation of the first hybrid tea in the mid-nineteenth century. These old roses were often overlooked at the time because people were enamored with the impressive flowers of the recently introduced hybrid teas. In the numerous articles he wrote for the *American Rose Annual*, Caparn constantly reminded his readers that while the new roses were spectacular in bloom, they lacked beautiful foliage, and that the overall appearance of a rosebush is just as important to the composition of a garden as its flowers.

Continuous beds of the wild and old garden roses that Caparn championed surround the central area of the Cranford Rose Garden. Other roses of historic importance grow infor-

mally in the triangular section to the south of the pavilion. Most of the old roses bloom only once, in late spring or in early summer, but they are eye-catching throughout the season because of the varying colors and textures of their foliage, prickles and hips. Massed together, they form a lush frame for the center of the garden, which consists of fifteen large rectangular beds — arranged in three rows of five beds each — containing roses of more recent date.

In the original planting, one could trace the evolution of the modern rose by following the path that encircles these fifteen center beds. Classes of roses that were important in the development of the hybrid tea — Chinas, teas, Noisettes, and Bourbons — were planted at the north end. These were followed by all the hybrid teas known in 1927, arranged in chronological order in the two outside rows, beginning with 'La France', the first rose to be recognized in that

*Below:* The pond in the Rose
Arc in a pre-construction
illustration and as it is today.
*Right:* View from the
overlook.

class. The five beds in the center row contained hybrid perpetuals and polyanthas, another new class of rose that had been developed in the late nineteenth century.

This chronological plan was soon abandoned because most of the tea roses and many of the early hybrids, which were too tender for the northern climate, died during the first winter. Over successive seasons, many hybrid teas died and could not be replaced. In addition, the Chinas, Bourbons, and Noisettes, which have awkward growth habits, did not fit with the style of the more formal hybrid teas, and they were moved to the border beds with the other old garden roses. Most of the hybrid perpetuals were eventually also moved to the old garden rose beds; the floribundas and hybrid polyanthas that were coming into vogue replaced them in the center beds. Today, the fifteen center beds, each of which is ten feet wide and fifty feet long, contain

as many varieties of modern roses as can be accommodated. Until recently, there has been no special regard for chronological order, but efforts are now being made to bring back varieties of roses popular in the 1920s and to grow some of them in their original locations along with other modern roses.

In the Cranford Rose Garden, where there are now eleven hundred species and varieties, the rose can be seen in all its various shapes and forms. The upright hybrid teas, polyanthas, and floribundas suit the geometry of the rectangular center beds, while other types of roses with more carefree growth habits are allowed to ramble, climb, trail, and spread. Climbing roses scramble up concrete posts, festoon themselves along chains, and swing up and over double metal arches spanning the gravel walkway that surrounds the center section. Old garden roses in the border beds clamber up cedar posts placed

*Left:* 'Pinata' growing on a pavilion window. *Below:* Mrs. Walter V. Cranford cuts the cake on rose day. *Far left:* 'Peter Malins, Rosarian' was the work of the world-renowned rosarian who was in charge of the Cranford Rose Garden for nearly thirty years, until 1983.

Visitors to the rose garden include a Russian rock star who taped a video here in September, 1989; working artists; our dedicated and hardworking volunteers; and thousands of schoolchildren.

between the wild roses, and beyond these, modern climbers and ramblers form a lush cover for the latticework that encloses the garden. On the pavilion, other climbers, including several that were developed by one of America's foremost early hybridizers, Dr. Walter Van Fleet, make their way up the columns and creep over the roof. Procumbent and low-growing roses spread naturally over the mound on which the pavilion is built. More climbers, ramblers, species, and modern landscape roses wander informally up the hill to The Overlook.

In 1936, after the death of her husband, Mrs. Cranford gave an additional gift so that an area to the south could be developed as an extension to the rose garden. This section, called the Rose Arc, is close to, but not connected with, the main part of the garden. From a road in front of the Rose Arc, one looks over a hedge of 'Curly

Pink', an important hybrid tea developed in the 1940s by the Brownells of Rhode Island, to a semicircular pool in which are reflected colorful masses of 'Clytemnestra', a rare hybrid musk. Three beds of ramblers and modern roses serve as a backdrop.

In keeping with the emphasis on education at the Brooklyn Botanic Garden, each rose in the Cranford Rose Garden has a label with its name and date of introduction. Visitors are encouraged to follow the historical development of the rose while learning about its many varieties and the best ways to grow them. They can also see that roses will flourish in any region of the United States, for here over a thousand varieties thrive in the polluted air of a city with hot and humid summers and harsh winters. The Cranford Rose Garden is meant to be an inspiration to all Americans as they choose roses for their own gardens.

*Left:* Arches of 'Ivy Alice' at the pond. *Below left:* A view of the walkway. *Bottom:* The steps of the pavilion. *Right:* A bed of modern roses. *Below right:* A group of old roses.

*The original plants in the Cranford Rose Garden were gifts from the following:*

American Rose Society, 4 plants in 3 varieties.

Bobbink & Atkins, Rutherford, N.J., 670 plants in 161 varieties.

The Conard-Pyle Company, West Grove, Pa.

Henry A. Dreer, Philadelphia, Pa., 304 plants in 72 varieties.

New Brunswick Nurseries, New Brunswick, N.J., 601 plants in 108 varieties.

The Rose Farms, White Plains, N.Y., 90 plants in 15 varieties.

Additional roses were later contributed by the American Rose Society; Brownell Rose Research Gardens, Little Compton, R.I.; Jackson & Perkins Company, Newark, N.Y.; Kovac's Nursery, Purchase, N.Y.; Traendly & Schenck, New York, N.Y.; and Jos. W. Vestal & Son, Little Rock, Ark. There were also many individual donors.

Among the major donors of roses for the Rose Arc in 1936 were Charles A. and John H. Traendly of Brooklyn, N.Y., and Henry A. Dreer, Inc., of Riverton, N.J.

3 Rose Varieties

CHAPTER

## 3

PART ONE: *Rose Varieties: Species Roses*

here are at least two hundred types of wild roses in the world. We call these species roses, the roses that occur naturally and from which all other rose varieties are derived. Their simple flowers are usually composed of five petals, and they bloom once a year, in the spring. Wild rose blossoms, which are very fragrant, look much like apple, raspberry, or strawberry blossoms, which is not surprising since they belong to the same family, Rosaceae.

Species roses occur throughout the northern hemisphere. They grow in the intense cold of arctic regions and in the hot climates of North Africa, Mexico, India, and the Philippines. Many of them come from western China and central Asia. Fewer are native to Europe and North America, but they can be found in each of the forty-eight contiguous states and Alaska. In addition to these, many foreign species roses have been introduced to this country, especially through the efforts of the Arnold Arboretum in Massachusetts.

Species roses have been evolving for at least sixty million years, and they are able to sur-

vive in all climates and soils. Because they are freely suckering (i.e., they spread on their own root systems), they take up too much space to be planted in small gardens, but they make good borders, screens, and hedges, and if they get a good dose of sun in the spring, they will grow well in places that are shady for the rest of the season. Some, like the rugosa rose, have spectacular hips and colorful fall foliage.

Because the species roses are carefree, disease resistant, and winter hardy, hybridizers searching for new varieties of garden roses have experimented with many of them, especially *R. rugosa* and *R. wichuraiana* from Japan and *R. setigera* from North America, trying to combine their hardiness with the everblooming qualities of modern varieties.

Species roses are valuable in the garden for many reasons. They bloom so early in the season that they are not affected by insects, such as Japanese beetles, which attack during the summer; they don't need fertilizer or spray; and they don't have to be pruned unless they become overcrowded, invasive, or too large. After their flowers and hips are gone, the oldest wood can be

*Above:* 'Sarah van Fleet'. *Opposite:* Redouté's illustration of *R. Eglanteria*

*Rosa Eglanteria.*                    *Rosier Eglantier.*

Imprimerie de Rémond
= 2 =

P. J. Redouté pinx.                    Langlois sculp.

### Greenmantle

**(Penzance, 1895).** *Single, rosy red flowers with white eyes. Light fragrance. Often reblooms in the fall. Canes over eight feet long.*

### Anne of Geierstein

**(Penzance, 1894).** *Distinctive orange-red flowers with abundant yellow stamens appear to have golden eyes. One of the most fragrant eglantine hybrids. Sets bright red hips. Makes a handsome shrub.*

### Julia Mannering

**(Penzance, 1895).** *Light pink single, or semidouble, flowers with noticeable dark pink veins. Flowers and foliage wonderfully fragrant.*

### Lady Penzance

**(Penzance, 1894).** *A cross between* R. eglanteria *and* R. foetida bicolor. *Flowers coppery salmon with yellow centers. Leaves have the delicious sweetbrier apple scent.*

thinned out, and they can be cut back to any shape with hedge shears; they don't require the same careful pruning as hybrid teas and other modern roses. The best time to prune these roses is when they are dormant, as many of them bloom on both new and old wood; but a species rose that gets out of hand can be cut back at any time during the season. Some varieties, such as rugosas, will benefit from the removal of one-third of the old wood because the new wood produces better flowers.

Harold Caparn, the designer of the Cranford Rose Garden, thought the species roses the most beautiful and interesting of all the roses, and because of this — as well as the fact that they are the ancestors of the other roses in the garden — he had many varieties planted in the border beds, where they frame and set off their offspring. They are the first roses to bloom in the spring, before the modern hybrids; after they show off their profuse blossoms, they enhance the garden for the rest of the season with their varied foliage, colorful hips, and distinctive prickles.

*Rosa eglanteria* (formerly *Rosa rubiginosa*), the eglantine or Sweetbrier Rose, heralds the rose season. Early in the spring, its leaves begin to break and there is a spicy scent of apples in the air. When the eglantine's leaves are brushed against or touched by dew and spring rains, oil glands on their undersides release this delightful fragrance, which is present from the middle of April to the end of the rose season.

The eglantines are actually among the last species roses to flower: in June the buds start to break, and at the peak of the rose season they are in full bloom. The flowers, occurring singly or in clusters, are pale pink with white centers. Though not spectacular, they are very fragrant. In autumn their abundant, bright red hips delight birds as well as visitors to the Cranford Garden.

The eglantine and its hybrids are large arching shrubs, sometimes reaching ten feet in height, that are too large and thorny for small gardens. Because of their height and their menacing prickles, they can be planted in masses to create intruder-proof barriers, and they make excellent hedges that can be kept in check by pruning. If they become too dense, they can be thinned in

winter to remove the crowded inner wood and crossing branches. After blooming, the bushes may be cut back severely to promote the new growth that gives off the strongest apple fragrance, although this is not vital to the health of the bush.

In the 1890s, Lord Penzance, an English judge, raised a number of eglantine hybrids. Known as Penzance hybrids, most of these are the result of crossing the eglantine with hybrid perpetuals, Bourbons, or other species roses. Many of the Penzance hybrids bear the names of charac-

## Eglantine

The eglantine, or sweetbrier rose, is native to England and Europe, where it has long been praised by poets. One of the most famous references to it is in Shakespeare's *A Midsummer-Night's Dream*, where Oberon describes Titania's bower:

*I know a bank where the wild thyme blows,*
*Where oxlips and the nodding violet grows;*
*Quite over-canopied with luscious woodbine,*
*With sweet musk-roses and with eglantine.*

The eglantine was one of the flowers the colonists brought to the New World, and it has become naturalized in the eastern part of the United States. John Josselyn, a seventeenth-century Englishman who wrote about the plants and animals he saw on his travels in the New World, described how to make an eglantine hedge in *An Account of Two Voyages to New-England*, published in 1674:

*Eglantine or sweet Brier is best sowen with Juniper-berries, two or three to one Eglantine-berry put into a hole made with a stick, the next year separate and remove them to your banks, in three years time they will make a hedge as high as a man, which you may keep thick and handsome with cutting.*

### *Rosa carolina*

**The  Pasture Rose  (introduced 1826).** *Pink flowers borne singly or in clusters of two, three, or more. Blooms on both new and old growth. Very fragrant. Stems have distinctive pairs of straight prickles at each node. Foliage orange and yellow in the fall. Extremely hardy.*

### *Rosa hugonis*

**Father Hugo's Rose  (introduced 1899).** *Abundant deep yellow flowers on graceful, arching branches. Not very fragrant. Can grow up to eight feet tall. Hardy everywhere in the United States.*

### *Rosa x pteragonis*

**(Introduced 1938).** *Flowers bloom in a glowing, light canary yellow mass. No distinctive fragrance. Tiny, fernlike leaves. Huge, translucent red prickles.*

### *Rosa davurica*

**(Introduced 1910).** *Very fragrant, blush pink flowers. Foliage very light green, turning yellow in fall. Small orange hips. Dark, wine-colored canes. Freely suckering. Extremely vigorous and hardy.*

## Rosa primula

**(Introduced 1910).** *Yellow flowers. Fragrant foliage. Compact growth habit. Hardy.*

## Rosa spinosissima altaica

**(Introduced 1820).** *Large, creamy white flowers with overlapping petals. Very fragrant. Dense, fernlike foliage. Compound leaves composed of seven to thirteen leaflets. Suckers freely. Blooms in partial shade or full sun. Dark hips.*

## Frühlingsgold

**(Kordes, 1937; introduced by Bobbink & Atkins, 1951; 'Joanna Hill' x 'R. spinosissima hispida').** *Scarlet tinted buds. Sweetly scented yellow flowers. Grows up to eight feet tall. Makes a good hedge.*

## Frühlingsmorgen

**(Kordes, 1942; ['E. G. Hill' x 'Cathrine Kordes'] x R. spinosissima altaica).** *Large, lavender-pink and yellow flowers. Fragrant. Large shrub that can be trained on a pillar.*

'Harison's Yellow' in the Cranford Rose Garden. Species roses growing naturally tend to be large and full, commanding a lot of space.

ters in the novels of Sir Walter Scott.

After the leaves of the eglantines appear, the other species in the Cranford Rose Garden begin to bloom. The first is *Rosa carolina*, the Pasture Rose, which flowers throughout the month of May. This short bush is native to the east coast of North America, ranging from Nova Scotia to Texas. *R. carolina* makes a good hedge or screen because it spreads freely on its suckers. When left on its own or in the wild, it grows about three feet high; but when it is carefully tended, as in the Cranford Rose Garden, it can reach up to six feet. No matter where it grows, it is virtually carefree, requiring no spraying or pampering. It doesn't set good hips, so it can be pruned after flowering without damage to its appearance. In winter, cut back the old wood to promote new growth the following spring. Remove invasive suckers.

Another early blooming rose, *Rosa hugonis*, or Father Hugo's Rose, is one of the species roses introduced to the United States through the Arnold Arboretum. It was named for the Reverend Hugh Scallan (Pater Hugo), who discovered it in China in 1899. Caparn included at least six specimens of this rose, which is also known as the Golden Rose of China, in the original border plantings in the Cranford Rose Garden. In some climates it grows very tall, but here it is a small, compact shrub that stays close to the ground. Unlike most species roses, Father Hugo's Rose is not particularly fragrant, and it does not produce good hips. No pruning is required except for the removal of any old, crowded, or dead wood.

*Rosa* x *pteragonis*, which blooms at the same time as Father Hugo's Rose in the Cranford Garden, is a beautiful shrub with masses of light yellow flowers from early May through June. Although the flowers of *R.* x *pteragonis* have the five petals typical of most wild roses, it is a hybrid that belongs to a complex group of species roses, many of which have flowers with only four petals, such as *Rosa sericea*, the Himalayan Rose. These roses are often grown as hedges to deter trespassers, for they are armed with distinctively large "thorns"—beautiful jewel-like red prickles that glimmer like rubies when the sun shines through them. Frequent pruning encourages new growth so the canes will always be covered with these

## *Stanwell Perpetual*

**(Introduced 1838).** *Large, blush pink flowers, flat and quartered, with button eyes. Very fragrant. Small, fernlike foliage. Especially good flower production in autumn. No hips. Very hardy. Thrives on neglect.*

## *Harison's Yellow*

**(Introduced 1830).** *Double, yellow flowers on long canes. Light fragrance. Small, fernlike, spinosissima-type foliage. Very thorny. Grows over ten feet high and twelve feet wide. Suckers freely. Extremely vigorous and hardy.*

## *Rosa canina*

**The Dog Rose (introduced before 1737).** *Pink flowers. Light fragrance. Very thorny, with large, hooked prickles. Canes up to twelve feet long.*

## *Rosa x hibernica*

**(Introduced before 1800).** *Pink flowers. Fragrant. Strong hooked prickles. Red hips. Very hardy.*

wonderful prickles. The flowers are borne on old wood, however, so leave some of this to produce blooms the following year.

The wonderfully fragrant, fragile-looking, blush-pink flowers of *Rosa davurica*, which usually appear later than those of the other species roses, are borne on dark stems and canes. *R. davurica*, which is extremely vigorous and freely suckering, can grow anywhere, and it is probably the most invasive of all the species roses; in the Cranford Garden it has even managed to grow up through one of the brick sidewalks. It makes an excellent hedge. After it blooms and during the winter, thin it out and chop it back to keep it contained.

One of the most exquisitely dainty roses in the Cranford Rose Garden is *Rosa primula*, a graceful little plant with yellow flowers that resemble primroses. Discovered in eastern Russia in 1890, it is sometimes called the Incense Rose because its foliage, when crushed, smells like myrrh or Russian leather. It is not as rampant a grower as some of the other species roses, so the only pruning it requires is the removal of dead wood. In Great Britain, this shrub is so highly prized for its delicate appearance and remarkably fragrant foliage that it has received an award of merit.

The next major group of wild roses to bloom in the Cranford Rose Garden are the spinosissimas, roses that evolved from *R. spinosissima*, often known as the Scotch Rose. *Spinosissima* means "most thorny," and the name is accurate, for all spinosissimas are fiercely armed with straight prickles and bristles. There are many different varieties of spinosissimas. They became naturalized in America at an early date; in 1831, a bouquet of fifty-five types won a prize in the Massachusetts Horticultural Society flower show.

One of the most notable spinosissimas is *R. spinosissima altaica*, which was discovered in the Altai mountains of Russia. Two large displays of this rose, a beautiful, freely suckering shrub, bloom from mid-May through mid-June in the southern portion of the Cranford Rose Garden. The large, creamy white flowers, borne on large stalks, have carefully overlapping petals, and they are among the most fragrant of all the wild rose blossoms. *R. spinosissima altaica* makes a wonderful hedge with its abundant prickles and dense fernlike foliage that stays green all summer and turns yellow in the fall. It grows about five feet high and five feet wide, blooming freely on both old and new wood. The old wood can be thinned after bloom and during winter. Other than that, it won't need to be cut back unless it gets in the way; postpone any pruning until winter so *R. spinosissima altaica* can grace the garden with its lovely foliage throughout the growing season.

Wilhelm Kordes in Germany created a series of early blooming shrub roses that are spinosissima hybrids. Two of these, 'Frühlingsmorgen', and 'Frühlingsgold', are outstanding in the Cranford Rose Garden. 'Frühlingsmorgen', a combination of *R. spinosissima altaica* and a number of hybrid teas, is a large shrub with enormous, very fragrant, lavender-pink and yellow flowers. It makes an excellent pillar rose that blooms for the entire month of June and then produces astonishing hips that hang from the canes. 'Frühlingsgold', based on a hybrid tea and *R. spinosissima hispida*, is a tall, stately shrub that reaches up to eight feet in height and width and makes a good hedge. 'Frühlingsmorgen' and 'Frühlingsgold' do not sucker; growing in more treelike forms than some of the other species roses, they tend to become top heavy. When they are well established, after four or five years, thin the old wood and cut them back to encourage new shoots from the base as these will produce the best blooms. This can be done every two years.

One particularly popular hybrid spinosissima is 'Stanwell Perpetual', a constantly blooming hybrid that was introduced in 1838. This rose, which was Gertrude Jekyll's favorite, is thought to have resulted from a chance crossing of *R. spinosissima* and *R. damascena semperflorens*, the Autumn Flowering Damask, at a nursery near London. Its large blush-pink flowers with "button eyes" open flat and quartered—a clue that there is a damask in its heritage. The many-petaled blooms remain very fragrant all summer long, and their delicate pink color becomes deeper and richer in the cooler weather of autumn. With its exquisite flowers and its small fernlike foliage,

*Opposite: Rosa sericea*

*Rosa rugosa rubra*

**(date of introduction unknown).** *Sport of R. rugosa, with which it is identical except that the flowers are deep magenta.*

*Arnold*

**(Dawson, 1893; introduced in 1914 through the Arnold Arboretum; R. rugosa x 'Général Jacqueminot', a hybrid perpetual).** *Single, deep red flowers that repeat reluctantly throughout the season. Color of 'Général Jacqueminot', but foliage and growth habit of rugosas.*

*Madame Charles Frederic Worth*

**(Schwartz, 1889).** *Semidouble, rosy carmine flowers. Extremely fragrant. Low growth habit, reaching about three feet. Outstanding yellow leaves in fall. Now rare.*

*Agnes*

**(Saunder, 1900, introduced in 1922; R. rugosa x R. foetida persiana).** *Multipetaled yellow flowers. Delightful fragrance. Rugosa-type leaf and growth habit.*

## Schneezwerg

**Also called 'Snow Dwarf' (Lambert, 1912; possible R. rugosa x *polyantha hybrid*).** *Clusters of delicate, semidouble, pure white flowers with conspicuous yellow stamens. Spiny canes. Wrinkled, sweetly fragrant leaves are lighter green than typical rugosas. Orange hips. Once extensively used as a hardy hedge. Blooms under adverse conditions.*

## F. J. Grootendorst

**(de Goey, introduced by Grootendorst, 1918; R. rugosa rubra x *unknown polyantha*).** *Red flowers, borne in clusters like those of polyanthas. Slightly serrated petals. Light fragrance. Blooms all summer long. Compact growth habit but can reach four feet tall and six feet wide.*

## Sarah Van Fleet

**(Van Fleet, 1926; introduced by the American Rose Society after his death; reportedly R. rugosa x 'My Maryland').** *Rosy pink flowers. Wrinkled leaves, somewhat lighter than the typical rugosa foliage. Grows to eight feet. Good background shrub.*

## Flamingo

**(Howard, introduced by Wayside Gardens, 1956; R. rugosa x 'White Wings').** *Five-petaled, pink flowers with strong yellow stamens. Light fragrance. Blooms throughout the season. Foliage not as rugosalike as that of some of the other rugosa hybrids. Grows about four feet high and wide. Wonderful border plant.*

*Above:* A familiar scene; *Rosa rugosa* growing wild at the seashore.

'Stanwell Perpetual' is a spectacular rose in the Cranford Rose Garden. Like the species roses, it thrives on neglect. The only pruning it needs is the removal of dead wood.

A mystery spinosissima hybrid is 'Harison's Yellow', a cross of *R. spinosissima* and *R. Hugonis* or perhaps *R. foetida persiana*. 'Harison's Yellow', often misnamed the Yellow Rose of Texas, is actually native to New York City, where it was discovered in the 1830s by George Harison on his farm in Manhattan. Harison, a lawyer who was also an amateur horticulturist, noticed this double, yellow rose growing in his garden because it was extremely vigorous, hardy, and freely suckering, and he gave it to a New York nurseryman, who put it on the market. 'Harison's Yellow' became extremely popular, delighting rose growers such as Robert Buist, who praised it in *The Rose Manual* in 1844 as "the only yellow rose of this character that I have seen worth cultivating." In the 1860s, homesteaders took cuttings of 'Harison's Yellow' west, planting them wherever they settled.

Like all hybrid spinosissimas, 'Harison's Yellow' is just as hardy as the species spinosissimas. The only care it needs is thinning every few years to prevent it from becoming too dense.

One of the later-blooming species roses is *Rosa canina*, the Dog Rose. A common wild rose in England, *R. canina*, which has lightly fragrant pink flowers, has become naturalized in North America. This very thorny rose can be easily identified by its large, hooked prickles. It needs a lot of space, for it is tall and woody, often developing canes up to twelve feet long, but it can be cut back to a manageable size. Many old garden roses, such as damasks and centifolias, have *R. canina* in their ancestry. This rose has often been used as an understock for modern roses.

*Rosa* x *hibernica* may be the Wild Irish Rose discovered near Belfast in 1802. A species rose that resulted from the crossing of *R. canina* and *R. spinosissima*, this shrub shows characteristics of both parents: the strong hooked prickles,

*Opposite:* 'Dr. Eckener'.

51

pink flowers, and growth habit of *R. canina*; and the foliage of *R. spinosissima*. In the fall, it has red hips. *R.* x *hibernica* doesn't send out many suckers, but under cultivation it may grow over ten feet high and wide; and it needs plenty of room, for its fiercely armed branches are treacherous. When it grows too large, it can be cut back to any height and thinned of old wood.

The rugosa rose, *R. rugosa* (the rose with the wrinkled leaves), is one of the hardiest of the wild roses. It originated in Russia, Korea, Japan, and China and was brought to the United States in the nineteenth century. Rugosas have been naturalized in much of Europe and North America, where dense masses of this shrub (which has thick, deeply veined leaves, and canes heavily covered with prickles of varying sizes) grow wild in all kinds of inhospitable situations. Rugosas are often called Beach Roses because they are a familiar sight in coastal areas, flourishing in wind, salt spray, and dry soil. They thrive on neglect and cold weather. In Japan this rose is known as "Hama nashi," or "Shore Pear." Rugosas fare well in the polluted air of cities.

Wild rugosa roses have many virtues in the garden. The large mauve-pink flowers of *R. rugosa* and the white flowers of *R. rugosa alba* are very fragrant, and they are so long-lasting that they are often still in bloom when the hips appear.

The characteristic peeling bark of the Chestnut Rose.

These beautiful, bright red hips, famous as a source of vitamin C, are as large as cherry tomatoes, and in the Cranford Rose Garden they attract warblers, redstarts, mockingbirds, and robins. The leathery, dark green leaves of the rugosas are distinctive, especially in the fall when they turn yellow, orange, and red.

Rugosas need very little care, and they should not be sprayed with chemicals, which burn their leaves. The new canes they send up from the base every year produce the next year's flowers. After a rugosa has grown for three years, help it develop new canes by removing one-third of the old wood; this should be done immediately following the first flush of growth. Rugosas may also need to be trimmed back and kept neat and free of dense or woody canes and shoots.

Because of their hardiness, disease resistance, and readiness to hybridize with other roses, rugosas have been used by breeders to create many hybrid varieties. The flowers of rugosa hybrids range in color from white and yellow to deep magenta. A number of these hybrids grow in the Cranford Rose Garden, where their performance seems to improve as they age.

'Arnold', one of the first hybrid rugosas developed, has single, deep red flowers. 'Madame Charles Frederick Worth', another very early hybrid rugosa, and one that is no longer available in commerce, has rosy carmine flowers that usually open in late spring and continue on through the fall. 'Sarah Van Fleet' has rosy pink flowers, very different from the deep magenta that characterizes the flowers of the species rose. This rose, named for the wife of the famous American hybridizer Walter Van Fleet, is supposedly a cross between *R. rugosa* and 'My Maryland', a hybrid tea created by another great American rose breeder, John Cook, in 1908. Its color is significant because hybridizers had been striving to obtain rugosas with flowers whose reds were softer than those of the species varieties. On the other hand, 'Agnes', a cross between *R. rugosa* and *R. foetida persiana*, has very fragrant flowers that are yellow, an unusual color for a rugosa. 'Agnes' was used to create some important modern yellow roses. 'Schneezwerg', also called 'Snow Dwarf', is a pure white rugosa hybrid. 'F. J. Grootendorst',

## Conrad Ferdinand Meyer

**(Muller, 1899; a** R. rugosa **hybrid** x **'Gloire de Dijon').**
*Exhibition-type buds. Large, pink flowers with many petals.*
*Fragrant. Repeats well. Leaves more like those of hybrid teas*
*than rugosas. Grows well on pillars.*

## Max Graf

**(Bowditch, 1919;** R. rugosa x R. wichuraiana**).** *Pink*
*flowers with five petals. Small, shiny leaves turn yellow in*
*the fall. Red hips. Fierce prickles. Trailing. Vigorous and*
*disease resistant. An excellent ground cover.*

## Rosa x micrugosa

**(before 1905;** R. roxburghii x R. rugosa**).** *Light pink*
*flowers. Yellow leaves in autumn. Growth habit of the rugosa.*
*Prickly hips.*

## Rosa foetida bicolor

**Austrian Copper (sport of** R. foetida**; introduced before**
**1590).** *Intense orange-red flowers with yellow centers and*
*yellow on the reverse of the petals. Flowers often sport back to*
*the pure yellow form. Spectacular bloom from mid-May to*
*mid-June. Tall-growing shrub, often up to six feet. Leaves*
*fragrant when crushed.*

### Highdownensis

**(naturally occurring seedling of R. moyesii; introduced 1928).** Bright red flowers. Foliage lighter green than that of most species roses. Canes appear thornless. Irregular growth habit.

### Nevada

**(Dot, 1927; 'La Giralda' x R. moyesii).** Masses of single, white flowers, about three inches across, on short stems. May grow quite large. Dark, plum colored, arching canes can be wrapped around posts or trained on pillars.

### Rosa setigera

**The Prairie Rose (introduced 1810).** Deep pink flowers borne in clusters. Scentless. Extremely long, arching canes. Can be trained as a climber. Beautiful yellow-orange foliage and clustered red hips in the fall.

### Baltimore Belle

**(Feast, 1843; probably R. setigera x a Noisette).** Very double, pale pink flowers in large clusters. Fragrant. Blooms once in the summer. Not as hardy as R. setigera.

'Highdownensis' is one of the few true red species roses.

which has a polyantha as one of its parents, is a very unusual-looking rugosa with small clusters of red flowers that look like carnations because of their slightly serrated petals. 'Flamingo' has five-petaled pink flowers; one of its parents was 'White Wings', a five-petaled hybrid tea created in 1947.

Some rugosa hybrids, such as 'Conrad Ferdinand Meyer', can be grown as pillars. This rose has exhibition-type buds and beautiful, large, fragrant, many-petaled pink flowers, which it probably inherited from its tea rose parent, 'Gloire de Dijon'. Wrapped around a ten-foot pillar in the Cranford Garden, it is a wonderful sight when it is in full bloom. Because 'Conrad Ferdinand Meyer' repeats its bloom, it should be deadheaded back to the first set of leaves to promote new flowers.

'Max Graf' is a procumbent rugosa hybrid. Discovered in a private garden in Connecticut, it is the result of a natural crossing of *R. rugosa* and *R. wichuraiana*, a trailing rose with small shiny leaves and fierce prickles. 'Max Graf' has flowers that resemble those of the species

rugosas but the growth habit of the wichuraianas—which makes it valuable as a vigorous and disease-free ground cover, excellent for planting on mounds and embankments. Its only fault is that, as one rosarian has remarked, it has to be pruned by someone wearing boxing gloves. This is not a serious drawback, however, as it does perfectly well on its own. In 1951 'Max Graf' became the parent of *Rosa kordesii*, a rose that was the forerunner of a new breed of hardy climbers and shrubs combining all the best qualities of *R. rugosa* and *R. wichuraiana*.

*Rosa* x *micrugosa* is a species hybrid resulting from the crossing of *R. rugosa* and *R. roxburghii*. The latter is known as the Chestnut Rose because it has extremely bristly hips that resemble chestnuts. *R.* x *micrugosa* has the prickly hips of the Chestnut Rose and the flowers and growth habit of a rugosa. It is pruned in the same manner as the rugosas.

The Chestnut Rose is an unusual wild rose whose older wood has shaggy peeling bark like that of an old, gnarled birch tree. This unusual bark, which gets more attractive with age

and is particularly noticeable in the fall, is part of *R. roxburghii*'s charm, and so it should be pruned more carefully than other species roses.

Opposite the yellow hybrid rugosa 'Agnes', at the other end of the Cranford Rose Garden, are her forebears, the foetidas. *Rosa foetida*, a tall-growing shrub with pure yellow, five-petaled flowers, is often called Austrian Brier or Austrian Yellow because it was known in Austria in the sixteenth century, but this wild rose is actually a native of Southwest Asia. As the name implies, its flowers have a definite odor, but opinions vary about whether the scent, which has been compared to linseed oil or musk, is actually unpleasant: some people find it very agreeable. *R. foetida bicolor* is a sport of *R. foetida*. This rose, known as Austrian Copper, was discovered growing in Europe in the 1500s. It has striking flowers—intense orange-red with yellow centers, and yellow on the reverse of the petals. This large, tall-growing shrub, whose leaves are pleasantly fragrant when crushed, grows up to six feet, putting on a spectacular show of blooms from mid-May to mid-June. Its flowers often sport back to the pure yellow form. Since it tends to suffer from blackspot and may be completely defoliated by midsummer, it looks best when planted in a sunny spot where tall-growing perennials or summer-flowering shrubs can hide its nakedness.

Foetidas are absolutely carefree and are left to grow on their own with only minimal pruning to keep them from becoming too woody.

The only species rose in the Cranford Rose Garden that is true red is *Rosa moyesii*, which has brilliant crimson, five-petaled flowers and exotic bottle-shaped hips. Up until the discovery of this rose high in the mountains of west Szechuan, China, in 1894, the wild roses that had been seen were white, yellow, or pink. Also growing in the Cranford Garden is a naturally occurring offspring of *R. moyesii* called 'Highdownensis'. This variety, classified as a shrub rose, was raised from a seedling in the garden of Sir Frederick Stern at Highdown, Sussex, in 1928. In our climate, it doesn't set hips as freely as the true *R. moyesii*. 'Highdownensis' has eye-catching, intensely red flowers. Its growth habit is more graceful than that of *R. moyesii*, but it is hard to train because it sends out long shoots that grow either straight up or straight out. It needs pruning to keep this irregular growth within bounds. The best way to handle it is to let it keep its taller, more interesting growth, and cut away the older wood at the sides.

'Nevada' is an outstanding hybrid of *R. moyesii* that has dark, plum-colored canes covered with masses of large, white single flowers on short stems. These delicate flowers sometimes acquire a light pink tint in hot weather. 'Nevada' may become quite large, depending on where it is planted: it can be left to grow free-form, or its beautiful, smooth, arching canes can be wrapped around posts or trained on pillars. Once established in the garden, it sometimes has repeat blooms.

The last species rose to bloom in the Cranford Rose Garden is *R. setigera*, the Prairie Rose, which bears its scentless, clustered, deep pink flowers at the end of June and in July. *R. setigera* is a native North American rose, discovered by the great French botanist and plant explorer André Michaux, who was sent on a plant-collecting expedition to the New World by Louis XVI in 1785. Found growing wild in the eastern and midwestern states, it is also called the Bramble Leaved Rose because it has long, arching canes like those of blackberry bushes. These canes may grow as much as twenty feet in one season. *R. setigera* can be grown as a climber, trained on a pillar, or left to follow its natural arching habit. In the fall, it has beautiful red foliage and wonderful clustered orange hips, so postpone any pruning to thin it back until winter.

The only climbing rose native to North America, *R. setigera* is the ancestor of a number of climbing hybrids, many of which grow in the Cranford Rose Garden. In the 1830s and 1840s, this species was used extensively by John and Samuel Feast in Baltimore, Maryland, to create a series of important ramblers, one of which was 'Baltimore Belle', whose other parent can only be guessed at because hybridizers in those days were not fastidious about record keeping. 'Baltimore Belle' is not as hardy as *R. setigera*, probably because its mystery parent was a Noisette.

*Opposite:* Rose varieties: White 'Schneezwerg', red 'Arnold', and an unidentified pink rose that appeared mysteriously on sucker growth in the Cranford Garden.

PART TWO: *Rose Varieties: Old Garden Roses*

he old garden roses are the classes of roses cultivated prior to 1867, the date assigned to the first recognized hybrid tea and the advent of modern roses. Old garden roses can be divided into two groups. The first group includes those that were cultivated in Europe before the introduction of everblooming roses from China during the late 1700s and early 1800s. In the second group are the Chinas and the roses they influenced, the tea roses, Bourbons, Noisettes, damask perpetuals, and hybrid perpetuals.

The pre-China old garden roses are the gallicas and damasks, the oldest known cultivated roses in the West, and the albas, centifolias, and moss roses. With a few exceptions, these are one-time bloomers, and their colors are generally white and various shades of pink with some striping and mottling. All the desirable fragrances in roses can be traced back to these roses, especially the gallicas and the damasks, which were grown in gardens prior to the introduction of the China roses.

## *Pre-China Old Garden Roses*

All the roses in this group grow best in colder climates where they have a period of winter dormancy.

### *Gallicas*

Gallicas are descendants of *Rosa gallica*, the French Rose, a wild rose native to either southern Europe or Asia Minor; the exact location of its origin has never been determined. *R. gallica* has long been called the Red Rose, but it is really a deep pink, not a true red.

*R. gallica* is probably the oldest cultivated rose in existence in the West, and it has an important place in history, for this rose, or naturally occurring hybrids of it, has been mentioned in literature since ancient times. *R. gallica* is no

*Above:* 'Königen von Dänemark'. *Opposite: Rosa gallica officinalis,* illustration by Redouté.

*Rosa Gallica officinalis.*          *Rosier de Provins ordinaire.*

Imprimerie de Rémond

8

P. J. Redouté pinx.          Langlois sculp.

## La Belle Sultane

**Also called 'Violacea' (introduced 1795).** *Vivid pink, almost purple, flowers open wide to expose brilliant yellow centers. Fragrant. Dark green foliage. Plum colored and orange hips. Spreading. Good background shrub.*

## Sissinghurst Castle

**(Reintroduced in 1947 by Vita Sackville-West, who found it in the garden at Sissinghurst Castle.)** *Deep plum-colored flowers with yellow stamens. Fragrant. Moderately vigorous.*

## Complicata

**(origin unknown).** *Large, single, pink flowers with yellow centers. Fragrant. Very beautiful, round, orange hips. Awkward spreading growth habit in milder climates.*

## James Mason

**(Beales, 1982; 'Scharlachglut' x 'Tuscany Superb').** *Large, velvety red flowers. Dark green foliage. Tall shrub. A new Gallica rose. Makes a large, spreading shrub. Good landscape plant. Prominent yellow stamens give "button-eye" look.*

doubt the rose Pliny called the Rose of Miletus in his *Natural History* and the rose the Romans grew in their gardens and used so extravagantly at their feasts and orgies. The Romans were also well aware of the medicinal importance of this rose, and they planted it wherever their military campaigns took them. *R. gallica*, which is extremely hardy and easy to grow, can survive anywhere. It was cultivated so extensively by monks and royalty throughout the Middle Ages and the Renaissance that numerous accidental crossings took place, with the result that there are now many different kinds of gallica roses. Gallicas should be considered the forefathers of all other old garden roses, and the modern roses as well. They were especially important in the development of the

hybrid perpetuals. Before the nineteenth century, the gallica was the commonest form of rose in cultivation; in 1848, William Paul, a prominent English rosarian, listed over five hundred varieties in his book *The Rose Garden*.

A low, suckering shrub with large, fragrant, deep pink flowers borne singly or in small clusters, *R. gallica* is a freely spreading, extremely hardy, and disease-resistant rose. It tolerates harsh conditions and thrives in very cold or very hot climates. Its flowers have five deep pink petals and beautiful yellow stamens. The leaves, which tend to droop, have a resinous scent when crushed, and they are coarse and dark green, like those of the rugosa rose. They are usually composed of three to five leaflets. The leaf stems are smooth,

*Rosa gallica officinalis*

The most famous gallica rose is *R. gallica officinalis*, the Apothecary's Rose. Thought to have originated somewhere in Europe, it is also called the Rose of Provins, after a town near Paris where it was grown for centuries for the medicinal preparations of druggists and herbalists. Gallicas and other types of roses were so important medicinally in medieval times that the Emperor Charlemagne had them planted in all the imperial gardens. One plan of a medieval monastery shows a whole bed of roses in the herb garden where the monks' doctor gathered the plants for his medicines. Roses were made into syrups, salves, oils, ointments, and rose waters for treating headaches, sore eyes, skin blemishes, wounds, dysentery, melancholy, and a host of ailments so numerous that one monk said no man could remember them all.

The Apothecary's Rose came to America with the Pilgrims, who used it in their medicines and for household purposes, and it has been naturalized in many areas of the country. In Virginia it is

often called the Offley Rose because plants were supposedly carried to Offley by the wife of General Thomas Nelson when she and her husband fled from the British at Yorktown during the Revolutionary War.

In his *Herball*, 1597, the British herbalist John Gerard explained how to make a medicinal conserve of roses:

> The conserve of Roses, as well that which is crude and raw, as that which is made by ebullition or boiling, taken in the morning fasting, and last at night, strengthneth the heart, and taketh away the shaking and trembling thereof, and in a word is the most familiar thing to be used for the purposes aforesaid, and is thus made:
>
> Take Roses at your pleasure, put them to boyle in faire water, having regard to the quantity; for if you have many Roses you may take more water; if fewer, the lesse water will serve: the which you shall boyle at the least three or foure houres, even as you would boile a piece of meate, untill in the eating they be very tender, at which time the Roses will lose their colour, that you would thinke your labour lost, and the thing spoiled. But proceed, for though the Roses have lost their colour, the water hath gotten the tincture thereof; then shall you adde unto one pound of Roses, foure pound of fine sugar in pure pouder, and so according to the rest of the Roses. Thus shall you let them boyle gently after the sugar is put therto, continually stirring it with a woodden Spatula untill it be cold, whereof one pound weight is worth six pound of the crude or raw conserve, as well for the vertues and goodnesse in taste, as also for the beautifull colour.

but the canes and branches are distinctive because of their bristly prickles—dense thorns that are finer than those of other roses.

Each gallica has its own blooming pattern and individual flower form. The flowers of *R. gallica* have only five petals, but some of the hybrid gallicas have many more. Their colors are mauve, pink, red, and blush white. The buds are usually round, and the petals either open up flat, exposing the centers immediately, or reflex back so that the flowers are globular or pompon shaped. Quartering is common.

Gallicas have wonderfully lush foliage. Those with single or semidouble flowers produce abundant hips. Most of their blooms are on older wood, and the flowers become more profuse as the plant ages. The only pruning they need is thinning to keep them neat as old wood builds up and gets too dense. When they have grown for at least two seasons, prune them after they have bloomed to encourage new growth for the next year's flowers. An occasional hard pruning will improve flower production. All the gallicas are very hardy and easy to grow.

One of the historic gallicas growing in the Cranford Rose Garden is *R. gallica officinalis*, also known as Apothecary's Rose. The famous 'Rosa Mundi', which was supposedly named after Fair Rosamond, King Henry II's mistress, is a sport of *R. gallica officinalis*. Also called *R. gallica versicolor*, 'Rosa Mundi' is an example of a gallica with striped flowers. It often sports back to *R. gallica officinalis* on the same bush. 'Rose du Maître d'Ecole' is another very old gallica growing in the Cranford Garden. This rose is now very rare.

Some of the gallicas make attractive border plants. Two of these in the Cranford Garden, 'La Belle Sultane' and 'Tuscany Superb', have wonderful dark green foliage. Their new canes climb up to six feet, while the older canes, which bear dark plum-colored and orange hips, cascade at the base of the plants like "skirts." These shrubs, which spread, demand a lot of space. Removal of some of their older wood in the fall encourages the growth of strong, upright new canes that flower and arch over the following year.

'Complicata' can be trained as a climber,
which is unusual for a gallica. The specimen in the Cranford Rose Garden, which was planted to fill in an area around an arch, unexpectedly climbed up the arch along with a rambling rose, growing six to eight feet high in one season.

## Damasks

Damask roses, the most fragrant of the old garden roses, are nearly as ancient as the gallicas, to which they are closely related. Although they are often said to have come from the Middle East, their ancestry is uncertain. There really is no such thing as a true species called *Rosa damascena*: all the damask roses appear to be hybrids that show the influence of *R. gallica*, *R. canina*, and *R. phoenicia*, a wild climbing rose of Asia Minor. Damasks have been cultivated for centuries for their fragrance and their medicinal properties. The oldest known appear to be Summer Damask and Autumn Damask. Long the only rose in the West that flowered in the fall as well as in the spring, Autumn Damask has an important place in the history of the development of remontant, or repeat-flowering roses.

The earliest records of the damask rose in Europe date from the early sixteenth century, when it was introduced to Italy and Spain by physicians, but it had been cultivated long before that. It was used to make perfumes, attar of roses, rose water, and a purgative liquor. The name reflects the fact that it was thought to have come from the region of Damascus in Syria.

Damask roses have very fragrant pink or white flowers that are semidouble or double. The more heavily petaled blooms tend to remain on the bush and rot: pinch them off after flowering. Damasks usually grow much larger and taller than the gallicas, and they have lighter colored foliage. Their fierce prickles, inherited from *R. canina*, are a combination of very strong curved prickles and glandular bristles. They need little care, other than occasional thinning and removal of dead wood. After they have bloomed for two or three years, an occasional hard pruning will encourage better flower production. All pruning should be done after the flowers have faded so new growth for next year's flowers will be produced. When the canes are cut back, the laterals

### Rosa damascena versicolor

**'Rose of York and Lancaster' (introduced before 1629).**
*Flowers either pure pink or an uneven combination of pink
and white, looking as if they had been dipped in white paint.
Very fragrant. Blooms in midseason, with no repeat.
Numerous bristles. Large, hooked prickles. Low growth habit.*

### Blush Damask

**(Introduced 1759).** *Slightly cupped, blush pink flowers with
deeper pink centers. Fragrant. Vigorous, tall-growing bush
with many bristles and small, hooked prickles. Not as thorny
as other damasks.*

### Hebe's Lip

**(Introduced before 1846, reintroduced by Paul in 1912).**
*Buds with red tips open to semidouble, creamy white flowers
with red on the edges of the petals. Vivid yellow stamens.
Flowers, clustered in groups of three to five, close at night.
Sets hips. Large growth habit. Long, downward-curving
prickles. Apple-scented leaves.*

### Mme Zöetmans

**(Marest, 1830).** *Blush-white flowers with pale peach pink
centers and button eyes. Almost pure white outer petals
reflexed, making full blooms look like snowballs. Upright,
spreading bush, very prickly and bristly, especially on new
growth and leaf stalks. Young prickles, bristles, and new
foliage tinted red.*

63

## Rosa x alba semi-plena

**The 'White Rose of York' (introduced before 1867).**
*White flowers with eight to twelve petals that open wide, exposing the yellow stamens. Tall, spreading bush. Very long, arching canes. Long, slightly curving prickles. Red hips.*

## Rose de Meaux

**Also known as 'Pompon Rose' (Sweet, 1789).** *Small, full, light rose flowers, quartered. Fragrant. Canes covered with straight prickles. Twiggy growth. Foliage prone to blackspot. Short bush about two feet high.*

## Königin von Dänemark

**(Introduced 1826).** *Very full, deep pink flowers borne in clusters of three to five. Blooms age to a darker pink. Foliage darker than that of some of the other albas. Growth habit spreading, not tall. Does not set hips.*

## Petite de Hollande

**(Introduced before 1838).** *Clusters of two-inch, very full, rose-pink flowers on single stems. Quartered. Sweet fragrance. Small bush with procumbent growth habit. New canes dusty green. New growth very vigorous and spreading.*

(the flowering branches) can be shortened by about one-third. Some damasks can be pegged down, which increases the production of laterals.

A number of the damasks in the Cranford Rose Garden have historic significance. The 'Rose of York and Lancaster', *Rosa damascena versicolor*, which may be a sport of Summer Damask, has bicolor flowers. According to legend, this rose symbolizes the union of the house of York (which had as its badge a white rose) and the house of Lancaster (whose badge was a red rose) at the end of the Wars of the Roses in England (1455–1485). The story is probably spurious, however: *R. damascena versicolor* seems to have been first described only in 1551.

*R. damascena trigintipetala* ('Kazanlik') was first noticed near the Kazanlik valley in the Balkan mountains of Bulgaria, where it has long been one of the main sources of attar of roses. Its pink flowers are extremely fragrant, and as the name *trigintipetala* indicates, they have about thirty petals. As the flowers age, the petals reflex back, turn light pink, and become rather messy before they fall off. The bush, growing three to four feet tall, is bristly, with an awkward growth habit. The large, hooked prickles that occur especially on the older wood are characteristic of the *canina* rose, which is one of its ancestors.

*R. damascena semperflorens*, also called *R. damascena bifera*, Autumn Damask, or 'Rose des Quatre Saisons', was the first rose found in the West that repeated its bloom in the fall, and until the introduction of the Chinas it was the only rose available for the creation of other repeat-blooming roses. Its fragrant, deep pink flowers, which have many petals, bloom in early summer and again in the fall.

'Mme. Hardy' is a nineteenth-century cross between a damask and an alba or a centifolia. This rose, whose flowers are possibly the purest white of all the old garden roses, was named for the wife of its creator, M. Hardy, the curator of the Luxembourg Gardens in Paris. Extremely vigorous, it can grow quite large and is best contained on a pillar or fence. In the Cranford Rose Garden, it is trained on a ten-foot pillar, which it completely envelops.

Hebe's Lip is the only damask in the Cranford Rose Garden with flowers that are not fully double. Probably a cross between an eglantine and a damask, it has the apple-scented leaves and large growth habit of the eglantine, although its long, downward-curving prickles are more numerous and more vicious than those of the eglantine. The buds of 'Hebe's Lip' have red tips that poke through the sepals, and the creamy white blooms have lipstick-like smudges of red on the edges. This rose was named for Hebe, the Greek goddess of youth.

## Albas

*Rosa* x *alba* is another old garden rose whose ancestry has been the subject of much debate. Now generally believed to be a cross between a damask or a gallica and a form of *R. canina*, the alba seems to have originated in central or southern Europe. It was grown by the Romans and introduced into England at an early date, possibly before A.D. 100. One variety, *R.* x *alba semi-plena*, is famous in history as the 'White Rose of York', the badge of the house of York during the Wars of the Roses in the fifteenth century.

Albas probably stand on their own with very little influence of other roses on their breeding, but *R.* x *alba* as a species is not known today. *R.* x *alba semi-plena* may be the closest to the species rose. In general, albas are extremely upright,

'Mme. Hardy' in the Cranford Garden.

65

## Old Red Moss

**(Origin and date of introduction unknown).** *Red, starburst-shaped flowers. Soft green foliage darkens toward the end of the season. Older canes plum colored. Tall, vigorous, spreading bush. Orange-red hips.*

## Laneii

**(Laffay, introduced by Lane, 1845).** *Very double, crimson-magenta flowers in clusters at the ends of plum-colored canes. Extremely mossy. Many bristles on the petioles and leaves. Prickly canes. Tall and vigorous. Does not set hips.*

## Salet

**(Lacharme, 1854).** *Round, tight buds open to full, flat, slightly quartered, rosy pink flowers. The petals, smaller toward the center, reflex and fade as the flower ages. Sweet fragrance. Buds, peduncles, petioles, and stipules encased in fragrant moss. Canes bristly with a few straight prickles. Vigorous, but tends to lose some of its dusty green leaves during summer. The only reliably recurrent moss rose.*

## James Veitch

**(Verdier, 1865).** *Buds show deep red through a soft, mossy covering. Small magenta flowers like starbursts in flat-topped clusters at the ends of the canes. Free-form petals reflexed and tinted with white at the bases. Very long sepals. Canes extremely thorny and bristly. Young leaves bright green with red edges. Vigorous. Grows to moderate height. Does not set hips. Blooms occasionally repeat.*

tall, and vigorous. They don't sucker like other old garden roses, and they have sparser prickles and tougher leaves that are a distinctive bluish green. Their flowers, most of which are fully double, range from white to deep pink, and they generally open wide and have good fragrance. The varieties with the fewest petals develop the best hips.

Because many albas grow very tall, they should be kept in the background in the garden. Like all the pre-China old garden roses, they don't need much pruning. If you do prune, wait until they have grown for two or three years because their best blooms are on second-year wood. As they mature, some of the older wood can be removed after they have bloomed to stimulate new growth for the following season's flowers. Once in a while, a hard pruning will encourage them to produce more blooms. The taller, more vigorous albas should be allowed to attain their full height and then receive only lateral pruning and thinning; these can be trained as climbers on low fences, wrapped around pillars, or left as huge shrubs. On varieties that are more procumbent, the older wood can be cut back regularly after two or three years. Albas, which will thrive anywhere, are extremely hardy and easy to grow.

Many of the older varieties of albas grow in the Cranford Rose Garden. One of these, *R. x alba semi-plena*, which is noted for its fragrance, has been used for centuries in the manufacture of rose attar. Plants of this and *R. x alba incarnata*, 'Great Maiden's Blush', have been growing in the garden for over sixty years, thriving in partially shaded areas in the borders. Until Victorian times, 'Great Maiden's Blush' was called 'La Cuisse de Nymphe Émue' ("thigh of an emoted nymph").

Many albas are good candidates for pegging. In the Cranford Garden, 'Mme. Legras de St. Germain' and 'Königin von Dänemark', both of which have a spreading growth habit, are grown in this way. The latter has exquisite deep pink flowers, and as it does not set hips, these very full flowers, which tend to stay on the bush after they have faded, require deadheading.

'Mme. Plantier', another very old alba, was rated in the 1890s one of the best and most popular white roses. At the turn of the century, it was often used as hedging in formal gardens. New specimens of this rose have recently been added to the Cranford Rose Garden.

## Centifolias

*Rosa centifolia*, known as the Cabbage Rose because of its globelike flowers, is thought to be closely related to *R. damascena* and may be a cross between the Autumn Damask and an alba. Because its Latin name, *centifolia*, means "hundred petals" (although it doesn't necessarily have that many), it has been identified with the many-petaled roses mentioned in ancient history. It probably originated in southern Europe or the eastern Mediterranean, but it was most popular in Holland, where it became a favorite rose of painters in the seventeenth century. It is often called the Holland Rose, and sometimes the Provence Rose, from the region of southern France where it was much grown, and this leads to confusion with the gallica known as the Rose of Provins.

Centifolias have often been compared with gallicas such as 'La Belle Sultane', which have similar drooping leaves, fall color, and growth habits. Centifolias grow much taller, however, and they have more prickly stems. Their heavy flowers, which tend to nod, are very fragrant.

Most centifolias don't set hips, and like the other pre-China old garden roses they bloom better on old than new wood. Their performance in the garden improves with age, so put off pruning until they are two or three years old, at which time any old wood that has become too dense can be cut out. It is best not to thin them too much, but an occasional hard pruning will make them produce more flowers on new growth the following season. Prune them after they have flowered. Tall-growing centifolias should be allowed to gain their full height and have only lateral pruning and thinning; if space is limited, they can be trained on pillars. Like the gallica 'La Belle Sultane', centifolias have very erect and vigorous new growth after they have bloomed. In their second year, the canes arch over toward the ground.

Because centifolias have foliage that is susceptible to disease, and large, many-petaled flowers that retain moisture from rain and dew, they should be planted in full sun; otherwise they are subject to blackspot and mildew.

One of the most distinctive centifolias growing in the Cranford Rose Garden is 'Bullata', often called the Lettuce-Leafed Rose because its leaves are very crinkled. It has the enormous "cabbage head" flowers one associates with the centifolias.

There are two very small centifolias in the Cranford Garden. 'Rose de Meaux', also known as 'Pompon Rose', is actually a miniature centifolia, although it is not officially recognized as such. The short bush grows only about two feet high and has diminutive rose-colored flowers. 'Petite de Hollande' is also a small bush, although its rose-pink flowers are not as tiny as those of 'Rose de Meaux'. It has a procumbent habit with very vigorous, spreading new growth. Its canes are pegged in the Cranford Garden.

## Moss Roses

Moss roses are sports of centifolias and damasks. Their calyx lobes, hips, and flower stalks are covered with a mossy growth that looks like aphids and is very sticky; when rubbed, this moss gives off a wonderful fragrance of pine or resin. On moss roses that have sported from centifolias, the moss is soft and green. On those that are sports of damasks, it is dark and bristly. Like the centifolias, the moss roses have drooping foliage that tends to mildew.

After the flowers of moss roses have bloomed, it is interesting to leave the unformed hips on the bush and observe their mossy texture. Otherwise, prune moss roses in the same way as damasks and centifolias. Plant them in full sun so their flowers do not retain the evening dampness that makes them susceptible to botrytis blight.

## China and China-Influenced Old Garden Roses

The wild roses and the European old garden roses (with the exception of those that have the Autumn Damask in their heritage) flower only once a season. In the late eighteenth century, however, a new type of rose was brought to Europe from China, and this was a momentous event in the history of the rose. For centuries the Chinese had been cultivating and breeding the many wild roses that grow in their country, and the hybrid roses they created had a very special characteristic—they were everblooming. Unlike the European roses, they bloomed more than once a season, putting out new flowers on every bit of new growth. The British who went to China to trade for the East India Company in the late eighteenth and early nineteenth centuries brought these roses back to England, where they were called Monthly Roses because they flowered over and over again throughout a season. (In America they were called Daily Roses.) This was the first time a constantly repeating rose was known in the West, and when the China roses were crossed with the once-blooming but hardier European roses, they revolutionized rose growing. The Chinas became the ancestors of all our modern, repeat-blooming roses.

The China roses were important for another reason: they brought new colors to the rose world. Up until that time, the gallicas had provided the only reds in old garden roses, and these fade to a purplish or mauve color. The red Chinas, on the other hand, are a true scarlet red, and they retain their color. In addition, there are Chinas with yellow blends and apricot tones that had previously been known only in some species roses.

The flowers of some China roses change color dramatically as they age and the pigments darken. *Rosa chinensis mutabilis*, the Butterfly Rose, for example, starts out creamy white and goes through several color transformations, finally becoming vivid scarlet. This characteristic, which usually involves a change from light to dark, has been carried over into many modern roses.

Some China roses are low growing, while others send up such long canes that they can be treated as climbers. In northern climates, where they die back in winter, they do not grow very tall. Some Chinas are nearly thornless, and some have very strong prickles. Their leaves are generally shiny and pointed, and their buds are

## Slater's Crimson China

**R. chinensis semperflorens (introduced ca. 1790).** Single, semidouble, or double red flowers, borne singly or in pairs. White at the bases of the petals. Light tea fragrance. Long, pointed leaves. Practically thornless.

## Old Blush

**Also called 'Parson's Pink China' (introduced, Sweden, 1752; England, before 1759).** Long, pointed, deep pink buds open to pure pink, loosely formed, two-inch flowers in a starburst effect. The outer petals darker than the inner ones. All the petals darken as they age, and they fall quickly. No fragrance. Long, pointed leaves. Orange hips.

## Rosa chinensis minima

**Known as 'Fairy Rose' (introduced 1815).** Small, light pink flowers, one inch in diameter, generally borne singly but sometimes in clusters. Sixteen pointed petals. Exposed centers. Very long sepals. Young stipules red. Strong prickles. A small bush, about one foot high, with tiny, pointed leaves. Said to be the ancestor of miniature roses.

## Rosa chinensis viridiflora

**Also called R. monstrosa, the Green Rose (cultivated before 1855).** Sterile reddish-bronze flowers composed of many petals that have reverted to sepals. Color deepens with age. Long, pointed leaves. Practically thornless. Irregular growth habit.

### Rosa chinensis serratipetala

**Known as 'Serratipetala' (Vilfray, 1912).** One-inch buds, crimson flushed with pink. Small free-form flowers look like carnations because they have fringed or serrated petals. Eight petals, crimson to light pink. Flowers at the ends of the canes. Tea fragrance. Leaves long and pointed. Canes nearly thornless. Erratic growth habit. Blooms all season.

### Eugène de Beauharnais

**(Hardy, 1838).** Large, three-to four-inch, deep purple flowers with more than thirty-five velvety textured petals. Very fragrant. Leaves less pointed than those of other China roses. Prickles straight and bristly. Compact growth habit.

### Hermosa

**(Marcheseau, 1840).** Rounded, lilac-pink buds open to light pink, very cupped flowers, one to two inches across. Twenty-five to thirty petals. Light tea scent. Bristly peduncles have a resinlike fragrance. Glossy, pointed leaves. Sturdy, slightly hooked prickles. New growth red. Above average disease resistance. Blooms constantly.

### Mme. Laurette Messimy

**(Guillot Fils, 1887; 'Rival de Paestum' x 'Mme. Falcot').** Long buds borne singly or in clusters of two or three open to nodding flowers with fifteen petals, pink with blends of yellow at the centers and darker pink at the edges. The loose, free-form blooms do not reflex. Tea fragrance. Long, pointed leaves. Blooms all season.

*Opposite:* 'Gloire des Rosomanes'.

long and tapered. Their flowers, which are on short stems, may have a light tea scent, but they are not particularly fragrant.

People were fascinated with the Chinas because of their ability to repeat their bloom and their unusual colors. But the flowers are relatively small, and the Chinas were crossed with other varieties of roses as hybridizers searched for larger blooms. These crossings resulted in many new classes, including the Bourbons, Noisettes, hybrid perpetuals, damask perpetuals, and hybrid musks. The flowers of these roses are often similar to each other, so for purposes of identification, other botanical elements, such as prickles, stipules, flower stems, hips, leaves, and sepals, must be carefully observed.

Because they are constantly growing and blooming, and don't lose their foliage, the Chinas and their progeny tend to have more disease problems and require more care than some of the other old garden roses. China roses flower constantly on new and old growth, and therefore they don't need pruning to produce new flowers. Careful pruning, however, will stimulate the best repeat blooms and improve the overall health of the plant. For maximum flower production, pinch off spent flowers to keep hips from forming. Chinas are evergreen and very hardy if the climate is right, as in Texas and California, where one finds centuries'-old specimens blooming nearly year round in cemeteries. In warmer areas such as these, where they never stop blooming, they thrive on neglect, growing quite large and needing only to be shaped to fit the particular growing situation or pruned to encourage new growth for flower production. If there is a moment when they are not blooming, that is the time to cut them back by about one-third. In colder climates they produce their flowers more slowly during the growing season and can be pruned in between periods of bloom. In these areas they also have a period of dormancy during the winter, and at that time they can be pruned back by about one-third to promote new growth for the next season's flowers. At the same time, remove dead and crowded wood, and shape the plant. Chinas will do well with no pruning at all, however, no matter where they are grown. They

are fairly hardy as far north as New York City, but they will also grow much farther north if they are protected in winter.

There were four important China roses: 'Slater's Crimson China' ('Old Crimson China'), 'Old Blush' ('Parson's Pink China'), 'Park's Yellow China' ('Park's Yellow Tea Scented China'), and 'Hume's Blush' ('Hume's Blush Tea Scented China'). These four China roses are known as "stud roses" because they were grown in the West for breeding purposes rather than for the beauty of their flowers or the appearance of their bushes: with the exception of 'Old Blush', they have lax and awkward growth habits. 'Slater's Crimson China' and 'Old Blush', probably the most important of the four, grow in the Cranford Rose Garden.

'Slater's Crimson China' was discovered in Calcutta by a sea captain who in 1789 gave plants to Gilbert Slater, a director of the East India Company, for his garden in Essex. It was not until a century later that 'Slater's Crimson China' was found growing wild in its native habitat, central China. This little red China, which is often confused with other China roses, has probably given rise to most of our modern red roses. In the Cranford Garden it becomes a small shrub with a very irregular growth habit.

In 1953, a rose in Bermuda called the 'Belfield Rose' proved to be a specimen of 'Slater's Crimson China'. By that time, 'Slater's', which was the parent of so many new roses, was almost impossible to find in the West. It had become naturalized in Bermuda, where it had been known since the late eighteenth century.

'Old Blush' or 'Parson's Pink China' is the other "stud rose" that grows well in the Cranford Garden, blooming constantly from early May to late frost. One of its names derives from the fact that during the late eighteenth century it was seen growing in the garden of a Mr. Parsons in England, but it had been brought to Sweden at an earlier date.

*R. chinensis serratipetala*, known as 'Serratipetala', has an interesting flower that is very similar to 'Slater's Crimson China' but smaller and carnationlike, with petals that are fringed or serrated. The buds, crimson flushed

## Mrs. Dudley Cross

**(Wm. Paul & Sons, 1907).** *Large, pointed buds open to flat, reflexed, pale yellow flowers that may have a flush of scarlet in cooler weather. Blooms occur all summer in clusters of two or three on single stems. Many petals. Pleasant but not strong fragrance. Nearly thornless. Does better in drier climates.*

## Sombreuil

**(Robert, 1850; 'Gigantesque' seedling).** *A climbing tea rose. Large, flat, creamy white flowers with a hint of blush in the centers. Wonderful fragrance. Fairly vigorous. One of the hardier tea roses.*

## Duchesse de Brabant

**(Bernède, 1857; parentage unknown).** *Large, two-to three-inch cupped flowers, soft pinkish-orange. More than forty petals. One of the hardier tea roses. Blooms prolifically in warm climates.*

## Mrs. B. R. Cant

**(Cant, 1901).** *Often sold as 'Reine Marie Henriette'. Tight, round buds open to very double, pink-to cherry-red flowers. Full, flat, nodding blooms. Light, delicate fragrance. Leaves not as pointed as those of other tea roses. Hooked prickles. Compact shrub sends up an occasional long stem. Blooms nonstop.*

Unlike other tea roses, 'Sombreuil' can be trained as a climber.

with pink, resemble miniature parrot tulips.

The most unusual China rose is *R. chinensis viridiflora*, the Green Rose. Also called *Rosa monstrosa* ("monstrous rose"), this virtually thornless rose has the long, pointed leaves and irregular growth habit of the Chinas, but sterile and scentless flowers composed of many petals that have reverted to sepals. These odd flowers are green with a reddish-bronze cast that deepens with age. Many people find this rose ugly, but it is attractive in a flower arrangement.

'Eugène de Beauharnais' and 'Mme. Laurette Messimy' are examples of Chinas that have old garden roses in their heritage and are often referred to as hybrid Chinas. 'Eugène de Beauharnais', which has a compact growth habit and leaves that are less pointed than those of other China roses, may have some gallica in its background. 'Mme. Laurette Messimy' has a moderate growth habit in the Cranford Rose Garden, where it blooms all season long.

## Tea Roses

The tea rose, *Rosa* x *odorata*, which is a form of a China rose, is thought to have originated long ago in China as a cross between *R. chinensis*, and *R. gigantea*, an evergreen climber with white flowers native to China and Burma. Tea roses were originally called Tea-Scented China Roses, either because their flowers smelled like tea leaves or because they picked up the fragrance of the tea crates in which they were shipped to England in the first quarter of the nineteenth century. They were much loved for their delicate colors, wonderful fragrance, and dainty leaves and stems, and also because they make good cut flowers. In the old literature on roses, they are often described as "refined" and "aristocratic," adjectives that may well have been applied to them because they are very tender. Tea roses, like the China roses, continue growing and blooming right into winter and either die back or are killed by the cold. The tea roses are even less hardy than the Chinas.

In warm climates tea roses make beautiful landscape plants. During the colder months in the north, they can be grown indoors in greenhouses or under lights and then set outside as bedding plants in the summer. They will die in the

## Coquette des Blanches

**(Lacharme, 1871; 'Blanche Lafitte' x 'Sappho').** *Pure white, multipetaled, fully reflexed flowers. Petals sometimes tinged with red at the outer edges. Blooms, sometimes in pairs, borne on long peduncles. Lightly scented. Bushy plant with pointed leaves. Vigorous. Very hardy. Good fall rebloom.*

## Boule de Neige

**(Lacharme, 1867; 'Blanche Lafitte' x 'Sappho').** *Tight, round buds tinged with scarlet open to pure white, double flowers that look like snowballs. Blooms occur singly or in clusters. Thirty reflexed petals. Projecting yellow stamens. Fragrant. Slightly bristly peduncles. Compact shrub, about three feet tall and three feet wide. Hardy and disease resistant.*

## Mme. Pierre Oger

**(Oger, introduced by C. Verdier, 1878; a sport of 'La Reine Victoria').** *Delicate cupped flowers, two to three inches across, blush pink with a rosy lilac tinge. Eighteen petals. Fragrant. Long, pointed, dark green leaves. Strong, slightly curved prickles. Upright growth habit. Vigorous. Subject to blackspot. Does not repeat its bloom.*

## Eugene E. Marlitt

**(Geschwind, 1900).** *Globular buds. Bright, carmine-red flowers borne three to four along a stem. Fully double and nodding. Reflexed petals. Centers cupped. Light fragrance. Extremely vigorous bush in warm climates, where it is sometimes grown as a climber.*

### Mme Cornelissen

**(parentage and date of introduction unknown).** *Globular buds, pink flushed with carmine, open to cupped flowers with about forty petals and exposed yellow stamens. Light-pink outer petals reflexed, dark-pink inner petals ruffled. Tea fragrance. Thornless. Rounded leaves. Moderately vigorous. Blooms constantly.*

### La Reine Victoria

**(Schwartz, 1872)** *Rich pink flowers, cupped and very fragrant. Upright vigorous growth habit. A popular Bourbon. Especially good for containers.*

### Souvenir de la Malmaison

**(Béluze, 1843; 'Mme. Desprez' x a tea rose).** *Large, urn-shaped buds open to quartered, three-to four-inch, creamy flesh pink flowers. Yellow button eyes. More than fifty dense, reflexed, and pointed petals. Spicy fragrance. Bristly peduncles smell like resin when rubbed. Leaves a bit more pointed than those of other Bourbons. Hooked prickles. Vigorous. Good rebloom.*

### Rosa x borboniana

**Also known as Bourbon Rose (introduced 1817).** *The original Bourbon rose. Clustered three-inch pink flowers. Twenty-five to thirty petals. Susceptible to blackspot. Repeat blooming.*

winter if left outside without adequate protection. One way to carry them over the winter is to bring them into the house in containers.

All the instructions for pruning China roses apply to the tea roses as well. In cooler climates they have periods in which they are slow to rebloom, and during these times they can be pruned back hard to encourage productive new growth.

A few of the hardier varieties of tea roses will survive the winters in the Cranford Rose Garden. 'Mrs. Dudley Cross', which has very full, pale yellow flowers, is a good tea rose for drier climates because the many petals don't open well in damp weather. 'Sombreuil', one of the hardiest and most fragrant tea roses, is a climbing variety that is fairly vigorous in the Cranford Garden, where it is trained on a lattice fence. It is also a good rose to grow on a pillar. 'Duchesse de Brabant', famous as the rose that President Theodore Roosevelt always wore in his buttonhole, is another of the hardier varieties.

## Bourbons

Not all the early hybridizing of China roses was intentional. One of the most famous cross breedings took place accidentally on the French Ile de Bourbon (now called Réunion) in the Indian Ocean, where hedgerows were commonly made up of two rows of roses, one of Chinas ('Parson's Pink China' or 'Old Blush') and the other of the European Autumn Damask, the repeating damask, which the French called 'Rose des Quatre Saisons'. The owner of an estate on the island discovered in one of his hedges a young rosebush that was different from the others, and he transplanted it into his garden. A French botanist noticed it and in 1817 sent its seeds back to France to be cultivated. Known as Bourbon roses, these roses are repeat blooming, but they have larger flowers than the Chinas, whose blooms are relatively small, and they are also more fragrant.

The Bourbons were further developed when the original varieties were crossed with gallica and damask hybrids. Many new types, varying in color from white to red, pink, and striped, and having many different growth habits, resulted.

There are several Bourbons in the Cranford Rose Garden. They have wonderful colors and fragrances, and in general they are excellent repeat bloomers, much hardier than their tea and China ancestors. Their flowers, varying in color from pure white to deep red and sometimes having brilliant stripes, look very much like those of modern roses. Their growth habit is somewhat like that of the Chinas, although not as awkward, and they are more adaptable to a garden. They often become quite large. Some of them can be grown as climbers and trained on pillars, while others make rounded shrubs.

Like the Chinas, some Bourbons are constantly in flower, and a certain amount of pruning will encourage abundant repeat blooms. Not all Bourbons are pruned in the same way, however. The original Bourbon was a cross between a China and a damask, but later many other crosses were made, and pruning depends on the heritage. Basically, when a plant is two or three years old and has sufficient growth, it can be pruned while it is still dormant, at the beginning of the growing season but before that season's growth starts. The most severe pruning takes place at this time, when the main shoots are shortened by one-third and all the others are shortened by two-thirds. Later, after the flowers have faded, cut the laterals back again by about one-third. Some Bourbons are procumbent and respond well to pegging, which produces more laterals and, consequently, more flowers. As the plants age, remove older wood. Some varieties, like 'Boule de Neige', bloom freely and tend to stay shrubby, not lending themselves to pegging. If these are simply deadheaded, they will bloom through the fall. Some do well pegged or trained as short pillars or free-form shrubs. The Bourbons are more affected by blackspot than any of the other old garden roses.

A specimen of the earliest Bourbon rose, *Rosa* x *borboniana*, grows in the Cranford Rose Garden. Another early Bourbon is 'Souvenir de la Malmaison', which was named for the famous rose garden Empress Josephine created at her estate, La Malmaison, near Paris. 'Souvenir de la Malmaison' is a vigorous grower with good rebloom in the Cranford Garden. Its exquisite, creamy, flesh-pink flowers have a spicy fragrance that was described in the 1930 Bobbink and Atkins catalogue as "strange" and "haunting."

'Zéphirine Drouhin' is a popular Bourbon that is grown as a climber. Each season after blooming it produces ten- to twelve-foot canes that look marvelous trained on a fence or a brick wall. In the Cranford Garden, 'Zéphirine Drouhin' grows on the latticework. This Bourbon is pruned like a climber: immediately after blooming, the laterals are cut back by two-thirds, and one-third of the old wood is cut out. Any dieback that occurs during the season is also removed. This rose repeats its bloom in warmer climates, but not in Brooklyn.

'Coquette des Blanches' is a very hardy Bourbon, considered one of the best everblooming white roses when it was introduced in 1871. Its pure white, fully reflexed flowers are like small white balls. It is a vigorous rose with good fall bloom in the Cranford Rose Garden.

The flowers of 'Boule de Neige' are also round; they look like snowballs. The buds have touches of red, as if they had been dipped in scarlet paint. Unlike some of the other Bourbons, the foliage of 'Boule de Neige' is not subject to blackspot.

'Mme. Pierre Oger' is a vigorous rose that grows upright, rather like a shrub, but if the canes are long enough they can be pegged, as they are in the Cranford Garden. 'Eugene E. Marlitt' is grown here as a shrub, but in warmer climates it does well as a climber.

### Noisettes

An important mating of a China rose and a European rose took place in America in the early nineteenth century on the rice plantation of John Champneys in Charleston, South Carolina, when 'Parson's Pink China' ('Old Blush') supposedly crossed with a musk rose, the white *Rosa moschata*. The result was a rose called 'Champneys' Pink Cluster', which is a climber like *R. moschata* but pink like 'Parson's Pink China', and repeat blooming. The William Prince nursery in Flushing, New York, marketed these roses in this country. Philippe Noisette, a French nurseryman in Charleston, sent seeds of 'Champneys' Pink Clus-

ter' to his brother in Paris, who called these roses Noisettes. Noisettes became the rage in France, and eventually they came back to America.

The original Noisettes were not very hardy. Some of the flowers, like those of 'Champneys' Pink Cluster', are very small; but as Noisettes were crossed with Bourbons, Chinas, and tea roses, larger flowers were developed.

Noisettes need very little pruning. When they are pruned, they are treated like the Chinas and the tea roses. Some varieties, such as 'Blush Noisette' and 'Champneys' Pink Cluster', which bloom constantly, shouldn't be touched at all except to remove faded flowers and old wood. Spent flowers are simply cut off back to the next set of leaves on the flowering canes. Vigorous Noisettes like 'Mme. Alfred Carrière', which grows like a climber and can be trained on fences and posts, should be pruned like the climbers. The flower-producing lateral branches that grow off the main canes are shortened by two-thirds.

In the Cranford Rose Garden 'Champneys' Pink Cluster' is not very vigorous, growing to about three feet and producing only a few repeat blooms after the first flush of flowers.

'Blush Noisette' is a nonstop bloomer in the Cranford Rose Garden, flowering right up to the first hard frost. In this climate it grows like a shrub, reaching only two or three feet. 'Fellenberg' is a short, vigorous climber that grows well on a pillar, sending out sprays of bright crimson flowers.

'Mme. Alfred Carrière', one of the more beautiful Noisettes, is a rampant climber, often covering walls and houses in warmer climates. In the Cranford Rose Garden its canes grew long enough in one season to be wrapped around a ten-foot pillar. It has large, nodding flowers on single stems, perhaps an indication that there is a tea rose in its background. This Noisette is beautiful in the spring, when it has massive displays of flowers, but it has only a few weak repeat blooms in the fall.

### Damask Perpetuals

This is a group of repeating old garden roses with a dominant damask influence evident in the appearance and colors of the flowers. All damask

## *Champneys' Pink Cluster*

**(Champneys, 1811).** *Large clusters of tiny, double, pink flowers. Slight fragrance. Moderately vigorous. Repeat blooming.*

## *Comte de Chambord*

**(Robert & Moreau, 1860).** *Large, very deep pink, cupped flowers with more than a hundred petals. Quartered. Deep centers. Petals not reflexed. Stamens and button eyes not visible. Fragrant. Dense prickles similar to damasks. Susceptible to blackspot and mildew. In damp, cool weather petals tend to stay closed and ball up.*

## *Fellenberg*

**(Introduced before 1835).** *Clusters of twelve to fifteen cupped, bright crimson flowers on long, smooth peduncles. Blooms one and one-half to two inches in diameter. Pointed petals reflexed to expose the yellow stamens. Tea fragrance. Long, pointed, shiny, dark green leaves.*

## *Rose des Quatre Saisons d'Italie*

**(Origin and date of introduction unknown).** *Tight round buds open to deep magenta pink flowers, quartered, slightly reflexed. Many petals. Long, bristly stems. Dark foliage. Very fragrant. Blooms early summer and fall. Damasklike growth habit and color.*

### Baronne Prévost

**(Desprez, 1842).** Large buds open to flat, deep rose-pink flowers, three to four inches in diameter, with classic quartering and distinctive button eyes. Very fragrant. Tough, disease-resistant foliage darkens in fall. Numerous strong prickles. Tall-growing. Flowers on short laterals. Benefits from pegging. Good repeat bloom.

### Paul Neyron

**(Levet, 1869; 'Victor Verdier' x 'Anna de Diesbach').** Enormous, very double, lilac-pink flowers resemble peonies. Extremely fragrant. Light green foliage. Long, nearly thornless canes respond well to pegging. Blooms nonstop from June until frost. Flowers sometimes ball up in autumn. The best hybrid perpetual for repeat bloom.

### Magna Charta

**(Paul, 1876).** Large, globular flowers, three to four inches in diameter, strong pink with darker shades of red. Numerous small curved prickles on older wood near the base. Large, spreading shrub with bushy growth habit. Dark green foliage tolerates some shade. Susceptible to blackspot and mildew. A few repeat blooms in the fall.

### Vick's Caprice

**(Vick, 1891; sport of 'Archiduchesse Elisabeth d'Autriche').** Three-inch cupped flowers, rose colored and distinctly striped with white and carmine. Very fragrant. Extremely vigorous and disease resistant. Good repeat bloom.

perpetuals seem to have the Autumn Damask, the only repeat damask, as part of their heritage. Traits inherited from *Rosa portlandica* are also present. The types overlap, and there is a great deal of confusion about how to classify them. Some are registered as Portland roses, some as damask perpetuals. In Victorian times, they were simply called Hardy Perpetual Roses. Here they are all included under the heading Damask Perpetuals, for they all have damask influence and are perpetual.

Damask perpetuals are pruned like the damasks.

*R. portlandica*, the Portland Rose, is said to have been first grown in the garden of the duchess of Portland at Balstrode Park in England around 1800. It became a popular rose in the early nineteenth century because of its bright red, repeat-blooming flowers. In the Cranford Rose Garden it is grown with the damasks to show how these two types of roses combined to create the damask perpetuals.

'Yolande d'Aragon' is probably a damask perpetual, although it is sometimes listed as a hybrid perpetual. The flowers are on short stems, like those of hybrid perpetuals, but the flower stems are very bristly, like those of the damasks. The foliage is similar to that of the damasks. In the Cranford Rose Garden it is pegged to produce laterals. It repeats its bloom through the summer.

'Comte de Chambord' is often classed as a Portland, but it has the light green foliage and dense prickles of the damasks. It is more susceptible to blackspot and mildew than other damask perpetuals.

'Rose du Roi' is a damasklike rose with dark, rough foliage. Portland influence is evident in the color of its deep magenta flowers. This rose will tolerate some shade, but it is not particularly vigorous in colder climates; it is subject to blackspot toward the end of the season. 'Rose du Roi' flowers on new and old wood. To get the best repeat blooms in the fall prune it a bit harder than other damask perpetuals, cutting it back by one-third after the first flush of growth.

## Hybrid Perpetuals

Portland roses, hybrid Chinas, gallicas, and Bour-
bons, all of which have old garden roses in their ancestry, contributed to the development of a rose, the hybrid perpetual, that became the rage in the nineteenth century. Often referred to as Victorian Roses, hybrid perpetuals are very hardy shrubs that bear large, extremely fragrant, many-petaled flowers on short stems. Their name is a bit deceptive, as they don't always bloom continually all season long. Unlike the flowers of the Chinas, which are smaller and sometimes have nodding heads, the flowers of the hybrid perpetuals grow upright, which made them ideal for display in the popular nineteenth-century flower shows, where they were displayed like works of art in "English boxes": their short stems were fitted into holes so that only their enormous blossoms showed.

The first hybrid perpetuals were developed in the 1830s by the French rose breeder Jules Laffay. Other hybridizers in Europe and America were soon hard at work developing new varieties, and their popularity soared, partly because it was widely believed that they would bloom all summer and partly because of their enormous, fragrant blooms. In 1844, the Philadelphia nurseryman Robert Buist had the highest praise for them, writing in his chapter on "Roses that Bloom the Whole Season" in *The Rose Manual*: "The varieties are yet limited . . . but a few years will multiply them to a greater extent," and in this he was certainly correct. Almost half of the nearly one thousand varieties of roses listed by H. B. Ellwanger in *The Rose* in 1882 were hybrid perpetuals (which he called hybrid remontants), and it is estimated that at the height of their popularity in the nineteenth century, there were between three and four thousand varieties on the market. One of the many hybrid perpetuals to cross the Atlantic was 'Mme. Ferdinand Jamin', a deep pink rose developed in France and introduced in this country as 'American Beauty'. Although this rose did not prove to be a successful garden rose—it was hardy and remontant only when grown in a greenhouse—it became popular with the cut flower industry because of its long, stiff stems. Even today its name is synonymous with red florists' roses.

At the time of their greatest popularity, hybrid perpetuals provided what people wanted

—large blooms on large bushes. But eventually hybrid perpetuals were crossed with tea roses, leading to the development of the hybrid teas, which soon became more popular. By the end of the nineteenth century, the hybrid perpetuals were almost forgotten, although knowledgeable American horticulturists in the early twentieth century, such as Horace McFarland, Captain George C. Thomas, and other contributors to the *American Rose Annual*, championed them because they are extremely hardy and well adapted to the harsh climates of many areas of the United States.

While there are a few white and light pink hybrid perpetuals, their colors are usually dark—deep red, pink, magenta, and even a borderline mauve. A few of them are striped. They don't necessarily repeat their bloom—this depends on where they are grown. Many varieties do repeat in the Cranford Rose Garden.

Hybrid perpetuals are vigorous roses that grow naturally in shrub form, producing large flowers at the ends of their canes. To prune them, thin out older wood and cut back all the canes by about two-thirds during their dormant period. Repeat this after the first flowering.

Some hybrid perpetuals grow as climbers and can be wrapped around pillars or pegged along the ground. These are popular ways to grow them because pegging and wrapping induce them to flower more abundantly, producing smaller blooms all along laterals that develop off the main canes. In the Cranford Rose Garden some of them are also guided along a low wire to create a hedge or border close to the ground. The first year that hybrid perpetuals are pegged or trained as climbers, they will develop laterals; shorten these by two-thirds after flowering. In the second and subsequent years, prune all the old laterals back by two-thirds during dormancy and again after the first flowering. Peg or train all new long canes that develop.

After the first flowering period, give all hybrid perpetuals ample water and organic fertilizer, such as manure, to further induce good repeat bloom in the fall.

'Baronne Prévost' is one of the oldest hybrid perpetuals still in commerce. The wonderfully fragrant, deep rose-pink flowers envelop the bush, which is typical of roses of this class. This is a vigorous, tall-growing rose with good repeat bloom that produces its flowers on short laterals and benefits from pegging, which is how it is grown in the Cranford Garden.

'Paul Neyron', one of the most popular hybrid perpetuals ever created, also has long canes that respond well to pegging. This is the best hybrid perpetual for repeat bloom; its enormous, remarkably fragrant, lilac-pink blossoms, which are often mistaken for peonies, appear nonstop from June until frost. In 1882 H. B. Ellwanger wrote of this rose: "The largest variety known, and a very desirable sort for the garden."

'Magna Charta', an important hybrid perpetual that was used in the breeding of modern roses, is a large, spreading shrub with a bushy habit that grows best in its natural shrub form. It is susceptible to blackspot and mildew, but it manages to survive these problems.

'Vick's Caprice', which was found in the garden of a Mr. Vick in New York in 1891, also grows best as a shrub. It is an extremely vigorous, disease-resistant hybrid perpetual.

The clustered flowers of 'Champion of the World' are shaped like those of their China parent, 'Hermosa'. This rose tolerates partial shade, but it is more tender than some of the other hybrid perpetuals, another characteristic it seems to have inherited from its China parent.

'Baron Girod de l'Ain' has unusual-looking flowers, bright red edged with white, looking as if they had been dipped in white paint. Unfortunately, this hybrid perpetual is not vigorous enough to perform well in Brooklyn.

'Frau Karl Druschki' was originally called 'Snow Queen' by its creator. In the United States it was called 'White American Beauty'. Both these names are descriptive of an important hybrid perpetual that is one of the whitest roses known. It is often classed as a hybrid tea because its flowers have high centers. 'Frau Karl Druschki' is a wonderfully vigorous and hardy rose that grows as a climber in the Cranford Rose Garden. It does well on pillars, and it can also be left to grow on its own. 'Frau Karl Druschki' tends to be damaged by mildew, and, like many white roses, it looks bedraggled after a rain.

## Champion of the World

**(Woodhouse, 1894; 'Hermosa' x 'Magna Charta').** *Clusters of bristly, pointed buds open to cupped, deep pink flowers with visible yellow stamens. Nearly thirty-five rounded and slightly ruffled petals that tend to reflex. Light fragrance. Pointed leaves. A few hooked prickles. Light green bristles with a faint smell of resin. Tolerates partial shade, but more tender than some of the other hybrid perpetuals.*

## "Hugh Dickson"

**(Dickson, 1905; 'Lord Bacon' x 'Grüss an Teplitz').** *High-centered buds open to large, cupped, clear red flowers with more than thirty-five petals. Exposed centers. Very fragrant. Tall and vigorous. Responds well to pegging.*

## Baron Girod de l'Ain

**(Reverchon, 1897; a sport of 'Eugène Fürst').** *Cupped free-form flowers, bright red, edged with white. Up to forty petals. Ruffled centers. Fragrant. Not as vigorous as other hybrid perpetuals.*

## Heinrich Schultheis

**(Bennett, 1882; 'Mabel Morrison' x 'E. Y. Teas').** *Large, heavy, cup shaped flowers, soft pink, quartered, and well formed. About three inches across. Very fragrant. Sometimes repeats its bloom. Not very vigorous in Brooklyn.*

*Following pages:* A basket of old garden roses.

CHAPTER

*3*

PART THREE: *Rose Varieties: Modern Roses*

*Hybrid Tea Roses*

If the hybrid perpetual was the rose of the nineteenth century, the hybrid tea is the rose of the twentieth. There is a great deal of controversy about the origins of this class. Some people believe that 'Victor Verdier', created by François Lacharme in 1859, was the original hybrid tea, but the rose generally accepted as being the first is 'La France', raised by Jean-Baptiste Guillot in Lyons, France, in 1867. The parents of 'La France' were supposedly a tea rose, 'Mme. Bravy', and a hybrid perpetual, 'Mme. Victor Verdier'. 'La France' is a long-stemmed, repeat-blooming, silvery pink rose with many petals and very good fragrance. It is here that the craze for modern roses started.

Hybrid tea roses combined the large globular flowers of the hybrid perpetuals, which have short stems, and the elegant long stems of the tea roses. They performed much better in the garden than the hybrid perpetuals, blooming more quickly and more often, and their longer stems made them excellent for cut flowers and for exhibition in vases at flower shows, where by 1918 they were the most popular class. The hybrid per-

petuals soon fell out of favor, and many were lost.

Hybrid tea roses have handsome flowers with high centers and the ability to bloom all season long. They come in a wide range of colors, and many of them are very fragrant. Some of the early ones, such as 'Captain Christy' and 'K. A. Viktoria', resemble the hybrid perpetuals. Around the turn of the century, another type of hybrid tea with five-petaled flowers was created.

Although 'La France' is fairly vigorous, many of the first hybrid teas were not hardy in all climates. Hybrid teas have always been very popular in the United States, but hybridizers are still searching for the perfect rose that can survive in extremely cold, as well as warmer, regions of the country.

Hybrid teas flower best on new growth, and they must be severely pruned at the beginning of the growing season to promote strong new canes that will produce large flowers on long stems as well as good rebloom. In general, the closer to the ground they are cut, the more vigorous the new growth and the larger the flowers. To get the best blooms in areas with hard winters, give hybrid teas a severe pruning at the beginning

*Above: 'Golden Girl'. Opposite: 'World Peace'.*

A bed of hybrid teas in the Cranford Rose Garden. Hybrid teas, the most commonly grown roses of the twentieth century, are especially popular because they provide beautiful cut flowers all season long.

### The First Yellow Hybrid Tea

One of the most important developments in the history of rose breeding was the creation of a yellow hybrid tea. Breeders had long been searching for a yellow garden rose, and this quest became an obsession with the legendary French hybridizer Joseph Pernet-Ducher of Lyons, France. Pernet-Ducher, an eccentric who was much loved by rosarians the world over, performed many experiments with the pollen of the yellow species roses, the foetidas. In 1900, he crossed *R. foetida persiana* with a seedling of a hybrid perpetual with red flowers, 'Antoine Ducher', and created 'Soleil d'Or', the ancestor of all our modern yellow roses.

*R. foetida persiana*, 'Persian Yellow', which is native to western Asia, is very much like *R. foetida* except that it is lower growing, later blooming, and not as vigorous, and its flowers are multipetaled. Its offspring, 'Soleil d'Or', has long, yellow buds and beautiful, nonrepeating flowers that are flat, quartered, fragrant, and deep yellowish-orange. This Victorian rose, which is classed as a hybrid foetida, is one of the parents of the first significant yellow hybrid tea, 'Rayon d'Or' (1910), strains of which are found in many modern yellow roses. Unfortunately, while 'Soleil d'Or' has extraordinary flowers, it is not vigorous or disease resistant, and its descendants carried with them the susceptibility to blackspot that plagues many modern roses.

# Hybrid Teas

## Victor Verdier
(**Lacharme, 1859; 'Jules Margottin' x 'Safrano'**). *Because this was an early cross between a hybrid perpetual and a tea rose, some rosarians argue that it was the first hybrid tea. Large, globular, bright rose flowers. More than fifty petals. Flowers tend to ball up in cool weather.*

## La France
(**Guillot Fils, 1867; 'Mme Victor Verdier' x 'Mme Bravy'**). *Considered the first hybrid tea. Long, pointed buds open to large, globular, silvery pink flowers that nod. More than sixty petals that tend to reflex at the edges. Very fragrant.*

## Radiance
(**Cook, 1908; 'Enchanter' x 'Cardinal'**). *Globular buds open to large, deep rose-pink flowers. Cup shape. Twenty-five petals. Long stems. Wonderful damask fragrance. Hardy and disease resistant. One of the most popular hybrid teas ever created.*

## Lady Ursula
(**Dickson, 1908**). *Dusty-pink flowers, lighter color on the reverse, nod like tea roses. High, pointed centers. Petals curled and pointed, reflex as they open. Strong tea scent. Very vigorous. Good cut flower.*

## Lady Alice Stanley

**(McGredy, 1909; parents unknown).** *Pointed buds with ruffled edges open to large flowers that are two shades of pink, flesh colored on top, coral-rose on the reverse. More than seventy petals. Fragrant. Moderate growth habit. Good disease resistance. Very hardy. An excellent bedding plant. Blooms all season. Good cut flower.*

## Irish Fireflame

**(Dickson, 1914).** *One of the early single hybrid teas. Pointed, spiraled pinkish-red buds open to delicate coppery-orange flowers with five petals. Fragrant. Moderately vigorous. Disease resistant. Blooms all season.*

## Red Radiance

**(Gude Bros., 1916).** *An important sport of 'Radiance.' Same form and vigor as its parent, but light crimson color.*

## Mrs. Charles Bell

**(Mrs. Charles Bell, 1917).** *A sport of 'Radiance', has the same hardiness and everblooming qualities. Also known as 'Shell Pink Radiance', which is an apt description of its color.*

## John Russell

**(Dobbie, 1924).** *An old-fashioned looking rose that resembles a hybrid perpetual. Large, globular buds on long stems open to vibrant, velvety red flowers with ball-like centers and rounded petals whose color darkens with age. Not very fragrant. Vigorous grower with disease-resistant foliage. Now rare.*

## Dainty Bess

**(Archer, 1925; 'Ophelia' x 'K. of K.').** *Single, lightly fragrant flowers, four to five inches across, on long stems. Five large, ruffled, deep pink petals. Distinctive wine-colored stamens. Constantly blooming rose with good, leathery, disease-resistant foliage. Very popular.*

## Grüss an Coburg

**(Felberg-Leclerc, 1927; 'Alice Kaempff' x 'Souvenir de Claudius Pernet').** *Large, round buds open to extremely fragrant, nodding, globular flowers with apricot-colored petals, pinkish on the reverse. Very vigorous bush of moderate height and spreading habit. Fairly good disease resistance.*

## Soeur Thérèse

**(Gillot, introduced by Conard-Pyle, 1931; ['Général Jacqueminot' x 'Juliet'] x 'Souvenir de Claudius Pernet').** *Elegant long buds, yellow, edged with scarlet, open fully to deep golden-yellow blooms with about twenty-five petals. Flowers borne singly or in clusters on long stems. Light fragrance. Bushy growth habit. Disease resistant. Always in bloom.*

## Mme. Cochet-Cochet

(Mallerin, introduced by Conard Pyle, 1934; 'Mrs. Pierre S. du Pont' x 'Cecile Walter'). Long, apricot-colored buds open to tea-scented flowers that blend apricot and pink in a free-form style. Twenty petals. Long stems. Good cut flowers. Attractive foliage. Now rare.

## Eclipse

(Nicolas, introduced by Jackson & Perkins, 1935; 'Joanna Hill' x 'Federico Casas'). Golden-yellow buds open to long-stemmed golden-yellow flowers with about twenty-five petals. Tea scented. Blooms open quickly and lose their exhibition quality but retain their color. Bush vigorous and tall, reaching five feet. Foliage susceptible to disease.

## Saturnia

(Aicardi, introduced by Robichon and Jackson & Perkins, 1936; 'Julien Potin' x 'Sensation'). Long, pointed buds open to free-form, starburst-shape flowers, scarlet on top and golden yellow on the reverse. About twenty petals. Fruity fragrance. Not very vigorous. Now rare.

## Miss America

(Nicolas, introduced by Jackson & Perkins, 1938; 'Joanna Hill' x 'S. M. Gustave'). Flowers flesh-pink with subtle hints of salmon and gold. More than sixty long, pointed petals. When fully open, the outer petals are reflexed and the flowers resemble dahlias. Exposed golden-yellow stamens. Strong tea fragrance. Good, dark foliage.

of the growing season, down to five or six inches from the ground. As long as the bud union is not dead, new growth will occur. Even in warmer climates it is necessary to prune fairly hard. A hybrid tea that is not pruned will send up new, quickly flowering growth that will be too weak to produce large flowers on long stems. Eventually the plant will get very tall, producing flowers only at the top. It will continue to grow until it wears itself out and dies because of crowded canes and the buildup of dead wood that invites diseases and insects.

When pruning a hybrid tea, remove cluttered wood and open up the center of the bush. Cut out all but a few strong canes. Each remaining cane should then be cut back to an outward-facing bud (buds, which produce the laterals, are the swellings that occur at intervals along the canes). After the first flowering, begin deadheading to promote good rebloom. Cut off the spent flowers and their stems down to the first set of five leaflets that points away from the center of the bush, or down to any leaf junction. (On some hybrid teas, such as 'Peace', the stems of the faded flowers should be cut back only to the first leaf set.) Continue this up to about one month before the first frost. The farther back the stems are cut, the longer it will take for the bush to rebloom, but the larger the flowers will be. In very cold climates, do not cut hybrid teas back for the winter, as this will create open spots and fresh wounds, sites for winter kill. Cut back only those that might suffer from wind damage because they are too tall. Save any serious pruning for the beginning of the growing season.

Hundreds of varieties of hybrid teas grow in the ten central beds of the Cranford Rose Garden. Their upright growth habit suits the symmetrical layout of these formal beds. Only a few representatives from each decade of the twentieth century are pictured here, including a number of important introductions by American hybridizers. Many of them are very hardy and are recommended for beginners as well as experienced gardeners.

'Radiance' is perhaps the best known of

'Friendship' is a hybrid tea rose that grows like a floribunda. Its ancestors include 'Talisman', a rose created in this country in 1929.

## Break o'Day

**(Brownell, 1939; Seedling x 'Glenn Dale').** *Tight, round buds clustered on single stems open to starlike, light apricot flowers with exposed centers. More than fifty pointed and reflexed petals. Strong tea fragrance. Very vigorous and disease resistant. Always in bloom. No longer available commercially.*

## Mme. Marie Curie

**(Gaujard, introduced by Jackson & Perkins, 1943; AARS 1944).** *Clear yellow flowers with high centers hold their color well. Long stems. Light tea fragrance. A vigorous shrub with very resistant foliage. A superb hybrid tea.*

## Peace

**(Meilland, introduced by Conard & Pyle, 1945; [('George Dickson' x 'Souvenir de Claudius Pernet') x ('Joanna Hill' x 'Charles P. Kilham')] x 'Margaret McGredy'; AARS 1946).** *Large, yellow flowers, often with pink and orange blends. Intensity of color blend varies, depending on where this rose is grown. Light fragrance. Distinctive dark, glossy foliage. Extremely vigorous.*

## Rubaiyat

**(McGredy, introduced by Jackson & Perkins, 1946; ['McGredy's Scarlet' x 'Mrs. Sam McGredy'] x [seedling x 'Sir Basil McFarland']; AARS 1947).** *Long, pointed buds open to large, deep pink flowers with high centers. Thirty petals, lighter pink on the reverse. Strong damask fragrance. Large, leathery leaves. Vigorous.*

## Lafter

*(Brownell, 1948; ['V for Victory' x ('Général Jacqueminot' x 'Dr. W. Van Fleet')] x 'Pink Princess'). Long, pointed buds open to free-form flowers, salmon-yellow, about four inches across. Twenty to twenty-five petals. Disease-resistant foliage. Vigorous.*

## Tip Toes

*(Brownell, 1948; ['Général Jacqueminot' x 'Dr. W. Van Fleet'] x 'Anne Vanderbilt'). Spectacular high-centered salmon-pink to orange flowers, borne singly or in clusters. Thirty petals, reflexed, opening flat to show yellow at the bases. Tea scented. Tall bush with spreading growth habit. Very vigorous and disease resistant. Now rare.*

## Curly Pink

*(Brownell, 1948; 'Pink Princess' x 'Crimson Glory'). Deep pink flowers, three to four inches across. High, rounded centers. More than fifty pointed petals curling outward. Extremely fragrant. Bush medium to tall. Vigorous and disease resistant. Makes a wonderful hedge that is always in bloom.*

## Forty-Niner

*(Swim, introduced by Armstrong, 1949; 'Contrast' x 'Charlotte Armstrong'; AARS 1949). Two-tone flowers, three to four inches across, with loose starburst form when fully open. Thirty to thirty-five petals, deep rose-pink on top, yellow-white on the reverse. Not much fragrance. Weak flower stems in fall.*

This bed of modern hybrid teas shows their wide range of colors, one of the reasons why they are so popular with gardeners.

the many varieties produced by John Cook of Baltimore. One of the most successful pink roses ever created, it won top honors in many early flower shows. Its sport, 'Red Radiance', became even more popular. 'Radiance', which is still a favorite rose with gardeners today, has grown in the Cranford Rose Garden since its inception in 1927, and some of the original plants are still here. Another of its sports, 'Mrs. Charles Bell', has the same hardiness and everblooming qualities.

'Irish Fireflame' was one of the early single hybrid teas, introduced as part of a group known as 'Irish Singles'. Its flowers are fragile, but they bloom reliably, preferring some shade and lasting best in cool, damp climates. 'Irish Fireflame' is a popular buttonhole rose. 'Dainty Bess' is another very popular single hybrid tea.

'Soeur Thérèse' is an important modern yellow rose, the offspring of two hybrid perpetuals and 'Souvenir de Claudius Pernet' an early creation of Joseph Pernet-Ducher, who was the first to develop hybrid yellow roses.

'Country Doctor' and 'Break O'Day', both of which are no longer available commercially, are important roses created by Dr. and Mrs. Walter Brownell of Little Compton, Rhode Island. The Brownells have worked extensively to create roses that will survive in sub-zero temperatures, and many of their roses grow in the Cranford Garden.

Contrary to the popular belief that modern hybrids lack fragrance, many hybrid teas are strongly scented. Visitors to the Cranford Rose Garden always say of 'Chrysler Imperial', "This smells the way roses used to smell!" 'American Home' and 'Patsy Cline' also have the rich scent of old garden roses, as does 'Jadis', which has an appropriate second name, 'Fragrant Memory'. 'Sweet 'n' Pink' is fragrant even when the buds are still tightly closed.

'Oklahoma', most famous of the so-called black roses, has velvet-textured red flowers that are so dark they seem almost black. 'Night 'n' Day', another "black rose," has fragrant flowers that are dark red with lighter shades of scarlet.

'Silver Spoon' is one of the so-called blue roses. Hybridizers have long attempted to create a truly blue rose, but so far this color has eluded them. Roses described as blue are usually purple or lavender, like 'Silver Spoon'.

Many of the hybrid teas are very easy to grow. 'Yankee Doodle', for example, an extremely vigorous rose that blooms constantly all season long, is a good rose for the beginning gardener.

## Helen Traubel

**(Swim, introduced by Armstrong, 1951; 'Charlotte Armstrong' x 'Glowing Sunset'; AARS 1952).** *Long pointed buds open to flat, high-centered pink-to-apricot flowers on weak stalks. Blooms are large, five to six inches across, and nodding. Fragrant. Dull green foliage. Tall, bushy plant. Fairly good repeat.*

## Country Doctor

**(Brownell, 1952; 'Pink Princess' x 'Crimson Glory').** *Tight, round buds open to six-inch silvery pink flowers with high centers. Petals slightly reflexed at the edges. Fragrant. Bush thorny, with very glossy foliage. Disease resistant. Now rare.*

## Chrysler Imperial

**(Lammerts, introduced by Germains, 1952; 'Charlotte Armstrong' x 'Mirandy'; AARS 1953).** *Large, five-inch cup-shaped flowers. Deep crimson. Forty-five to fifty petals. High-centered. Flowers tend to ball in cool weather. Very fragrant. Moderate growth habit and fairly good disease resistance. Old garden rose look.*

## Pink Favorite

**(Von Abrams, introduced by Peterson & Dering, 1956; 'Juno'; x ['Georg Arends' x 'New Dawn']).** *Large, fat neyron-rose blossoms with pointed centers. Twenty-five petals. Good fragrance. Always in bloom, but flowers tend to ball. Strong, light green foliage.*

### Aztec

*(Swim, introduced by Armstrong, 1957; 'Charlotte Armstrong' x unnamed seedling). Long, pointed, deep orange buds open to fire-orange flowers, four to five inches across, globular and high-centered. Thirty reflexed petals. Flowers often borne in clusters. Very fragrant. Spreading growth habit. Very disease-resistant foliage. Now rare.*

### Pink Peace

*(Meilland, introduced by Conard-Pyle, 1959; ['Peace' x 'Monique:'] x ['Peace' x 'Mrs. John Laing']). Large, deep pink flowers, cup shaped, quartered, and low-centered. Very fragrant. Petals lighter pink on the reverse. A fine, vigorous shrub.*

### American Home

*(Morey, introduced by Jackson & Perkins, 1960; 'Chrysler Imperial' x 'New Yorker'). Tapered buds on long, strong stems open to cup-shaped red flowers with about thirty petals. One of the most fragrant hybrid teas, with a rich scent reminiscent of old garden roses. Vigorous and disease resistant. Good, steady bloom all summer. Now rare.*

### Duet

*(Swim, introduced by Armstrong, 1960; 'Fandango' x 'Roundelay'; AARS 1961). High-centered buds open to flowers with twenty-five to thirty petals that are light pink on top and reddish pink on the reverse and have ruffled edges. Tall bush with disease resistant foliage. Blooms steadily all season.*

*Opposite: 'Electron'.*

## Carla

*(de Ruiter, 1963; introduced by Ball, 1968; 'Queen Elizabeth' x 'The Optimist'). Large, long-stemmed buds unfurl slowly to four-inch, high-centered, salmon-pink flowers with about thirty petals. Very fragrant. Exhibition quality. Tall bush with dark foliage. Vigorous.*

## Swarthmore

*(Meilland, introduced by Conard-Pyle, 1963; ['Independence' x 'Happiness'] x 'Peace'). Long, pointed buds open to high-centered, four-inch flowers in several shades of pink, light at the centers, dark near the edges. Light tea fragrance. Often wins Queen of the Show. Tall, vigorous bush with dark, leathery foliage. Always in bloom.*

## Oklahoma

*(Swim & Weeks, introduced by Weeks, 1964; 'Chrysler Imperial' x 'Charles Mallerin'). The most famous of the so-called black roses. Large, oval, dark red buds with points open to exhibition-type, velvet-textured maroon flowers, so dark they seem almost black. Four to five and one-half inches across. More than fifty petals. Very fragrant. Disease-resistant.*

## Casanova

*(S. McGredy IV, Fisions Horticulture, 1964; 'Queen Elizabeth' x 'Kordes Perfecta'). Large, high-centered, straw-yellow flowers on long stems. Nearly forty petals rounded and slightly reflexed, tend to ball in cool weather. A constant bloomer with strong tea fragrance. Long, disease-resistant leaves.*

## Lotte Günthart

**(Armstrong, 1964; 'Queen Elizabeth' x 'Bravo').**
*Ruffled, flat, deep red flowers with nearly a hundred slightly reflexed petals. Blooms copiously and vigorously, but has poor foliage.*

## American Heritage

**(Lammerts, introduced by Germain's, 1965; 'Queen Elizabeth' x 'Yellow Perfection'; AARS 1966).** *Long, pointed buds open to multicolored flowers, a combination of ivory, salmon, and yellow. As the blooms age, they become flat, while the petals change color and become yellow with touches of pink on the edges. Light fragrance. Vigorous.*

## Cherry Brandy

**(Tantau, 1965).** *Small, exhibition-type buds on long stems open to five-inch flowers that are full, cupped to flat, and colored coral to salmon, an orange blend that deepens in the center. Thirty slightly reflexed petals. Centers somewhat exposed. Blooms best in cooler weather. Dark, glossy foliage. Disease resistant. Moderate height.*

## Yankee Doodle

**(Kordes, introduced by Armstrong, 1976; 'Colour Wonder' x 'King's Ransom'; AARS 1976).** *Enormous, urn-shaped buds open to large, fragrant, cupped flowers, yellow-orange with apricot-pink centers. Over seventy petals. Vigorous, tall-growing rose. Tough, exceedingly disease-resistant foliage. Blooms constantly all season. A good rose for a beginner.*

## Miss All-American Beauty

**(Meilland; introduced by Conard-Pyle, 1967; 'Chrysler Imperial' x 'Karl Herbst').** *Also known as 'Maria Callas'. Enormous, very fragrant, deep pink flowers look like peonies. Fifty-five large, rounded, and slightly reflexed petals, some with a faint white stripe in the center. Old-fashioned-looking blooms, very full and cupped. Vigorous and disease resistant.*

## Night n' Day

**(Swim & Weeks, 1968; ['World's Fair' x 'Chrysler Imperial'] x 'Happiness').** *Another "black rose." Flowers have up to forty petals, dark red with lighter shades of scarlet. Fragrant. Moderate growth habit. Disease-resistant foliage. Good rebloom.*

## Maria Stern

**(Brownell, introduced by Stern's Nursery, 1969; 'Tip Toes' x 'Queen Elizabeth').** *An outstanding rose with four-to five-inch vibrant orange flowers, cupped to flat. Forty-five to fifty reflexed petals with deeper orange color toward the center. Spicy scent. Tall bush. Very disease resistant.*

## White Masterpiece

**(Boerner, introduced by Jackson & Perkins, 1969).** *Large, white, high-centered flowers with perfect exhibition form. Light fragrance. Extremely strong peduncles. Not very vigorous. Slow to rebloom.*

*Opposite:* 'Herbert Hoover'.

### Electron

**(McGredy, 1970; 'Paddy McGredy' x 'Prima Ballerina'; AARS 1973).** *One of the best everblooming hybrid teas. Exhibition-quality flowers, deep pink with thirty-two petals. Long stems. Blooms throughout the hottest part of the summer. Dark foliage exceptionally resistant to blackspot.*

### Vol de Nuit

**(Delbard, 1970; 'Holstein' x ['Bayadère' x 'Prélude'] x 'Saint-Exupéry').** *Large, high-centered, deep lavender flowers, three to four inches across. More than thirty-five petals. Blooms borne singly or in clusters on short stems. Repeats well except during periods of extreme heat. Low growth habit. Hardy and disease resistant. Now rare.*

### Mitsouko

**(Delbard, 1970; ['Michèle Meilland' x 'Chic Parisien'] x 'Peace').** *Large, round peonylike flowers with creamy centers and pink-tinted outer petals. More than fifty petals. Strong, sweet fragrance. Now rare.*

### Lemon Sherbet

**(Kern Rose Nursery, Ohio, 1973; a sport of 'Florence').** *Long, pointed buds open to white flowers with creamy centers. Long stems. A good cut flower. Spicy fragrance. Delicate, dark foliage. Vigorous bush, grows six feet tall. Blooms all summer long.*

## Medallion

**(Warriner, introduced by Jackson & Perkins, 1973; 'South Seas' x 'King's Ransom'; AARS 1973).** *Large pointed buds open to enormous, peonylike flowers, five inches across. Twenty loosely arranged petals, dark apricot with yellow bases. Strong tea fragrance. Vigorous bush, over six feet high, with large, disease-resistant leaves.*

## Jadis

**(Warriner, introduced by Jackson & Perkins, 1974; 'Chrysler Imperial' x 'Virgo').** *Also known as 'Fragrant Memory'. Elegant, exhibition-quality buds open to medium pink flowers with high centers and gently reflexed petals. Long stems. Heavy old garden rose fragrance. Large leaves. Vigorous.*

## Sweet 'n' Pink

**(Weeks, 1976; ['Prima Ballerina' x seedling] x ['Happiness' x 'Chrysler Imperial' x 'El Capitan' x 'Peace']).** *Deep pink, urn-shaped buds open to cupped, pink flowers, four to five inches across, with more than forty petals. Marvelous fragrance, even when the buds are tightly closed. Very disease-resistant foliage. Good rebloom.*

## Double Delight

**(Swim and Ellis, introduced by Armstrong, 1977; 'Granada' x 'Garden Party'; AARS 1977).** *Long, elegant buds open to large flowers, ruffled and peonylike, pinkish-red on the outside and yellowish-white on the inside. More than forty petals. As the flowers age, the white inner petals become strawberry red. Fragrant. Blooms well in autumn. A popular rose.*

## Pristine

**(Warriner, introduced by Jackson & Perkins, 1978; 'White Masterpiece' x 'First Prize').** Long buds open to classic, exhibition-form blooms with high, pointed centers and thirty blush white petals, deeper pink near the edges. Hint of apricot color in autumn. Strong tea fragrance. Makes a good cut flower. Foliage vigorous and disease resistant.

## Las Vegas

**(Kordes, 1981; 'Ludwigshafen am Rhein' x 'Feuerzauber').** Long, elegant buds, a mix of orange and yellow, open to large, orange, five-inch flowers that often nod. Twenty-five slightly reflexed, pointed petals, yellow on the reverse. Very fragrant. Moderately vigorous. Good disease resistance. Blooms constantly.

## Faint Heart

**(Mike Pavlick, 1980; 'Hawaii' x unnamed seedling).** Cream-colored flowers with about thirty pink-edged petals. Outer petals curl back to expose more pink on the next layer. High centers and superb exhibition form. Long stems. Good cut flowers. Strong tea fragrance. Nearly thornless bush.

## Honor

**(Warriner, introduced by Jackson & Perkins, 1980; AARS, 1980).** Long, pointed buds open to large, pure white flowers four to five inches across. Twenty-five petals. Flowers lose their tight, exhibition-quality form as they age. Not much fragrance. Tall-growing, not bushy. Poor disease resistance.

*Opposite:* 'Oriana'.

### October

**(Weeks, 1980; unnamed seedling x unnamed seedling).**
*Long buds open to high-centered, fire-orange flowers.*
*Fragrant. Upright, tall-growing bush with disease resistant*
*foliage. A good rose for cool climates; does not bloom well in*
*hot weather.*

### Blue Nile

**(Delbard, introduced by Armstrong, 1981; ['Holstein' x**
**'Bayadère'] x ['Prélude' x 'Saint-Exupéry']).** *Pointed buds,*
*sometimes in clusters, open to lavender flowers with thirty*
*loosely arranged petals. Not exhibition quality. Fragrant.*
*Shy to repeat. Bush tall-growing and spreading.*

### Madame Violet

**(Teranishi, introduced by Itama Rose Nursery, 1981;**
**[('Lady X' x 'Sterling Silver') x ('Lady X' x 'Sterling**
**Silver')] x seedling).** *Large, high-centered, long-stemmed,*
*lavender flowers with classic exhibition form. No fragrance.*
*Tall, upright growth.*

### Princesse de Monaco

**(Meilland, 1981; 'Ambassador' x 'Peace').** *Long, pointed*
*buds open to high-centered flowers with thirty-five*
*cream-colored petals edged in pink. Tea scented. A good*
*exhibition rose. Dark, glossy foliage.*

## Brandy

**(Swim and Christensen, introduced by Armstrong, 1981; 'First Prize' x 'Dr. A. J. Verhage'; AARS 1982).** *Tight buds open to loose, free-form flowers, deep apricot with yellow centers and lighter reverse. About thirty petals. Light tea fragrance. Bush has very straight prickles. Not very hardy or disease resistant in the Northeast.*

## Patsy Cline

**(Christensen, introduced by Armstrong, 1983; 'Angel Face' x 'Double Delight').** *Dark pink buds open to delightful two-toned pink, almost lavender, flowers, dark at the edges and lighter in the center. Strong old garden rose fragrance. Shy to bloom during the summer. Not vigorous.*

## Sweet Surrender

**(Weeks, 1983; unnamed seedling x 'Tiffany'; AARS 1983).** *Large, silvery-pink flowers, five to six inches across. Forty petals arranged in a cupped to flat shape. Extremely fragrant. Moderate growth habit. Steady bloom. Fairly disease resistant.*

## Olympiad

**(McGredy, 1984; 'Red Planet' x 'Pharaoh'; AARS 1984).** *Brilliant red flowers, cupped and slightly reflexed, on long stems. Lightly fragrant. Exhibition type. Disease resistant. One of the best red roses.*

### Miss Liberté

**(Christensen, introduced by Armstrong, 1984; ['Camelot' x 'First Prize'] x 'Gingersnap').** *Large, pointed, orange buds on long stems open to four- to five-inch exhibition form flowers. Petals salmon-orange, a lighter shade of orange on the reverse. Good fragrance. A vigorous grower of moderate height. Good, constant bloom.*

### Sunbright

**(Warriner, introduced by Jackson & Perkins, 1984; unnamed seedling x 'New Day').** *Large, flat, bright yellow flowers, up to four inches across, with about twenty-eight petals. Light fragrance. Constantly in bloom. Very vigorous yellow rose.*

### Silver Spoon

**(Weeks, 1985; 'Louisiana' x unnamed seedling).** *Tight buds open to large, high-centered, deep lavender flowers with forty petals. Not as elegant as some other hybrid teas because the flowers look too large for the stems. No fragrance. Bush has a spreading habit. Vigorous and disease resistant.*

### Milestone

**(Warriner, introduced by Jackson & Perkins, 1985; plant patent #5000; 'Sunfire' x 'Spellbinder').** *Medium red, cup-shaped flowers composed of forty petals with dark edges and a lighter reverse. Color darkens as the flowers age. Very fragrant. Always in bloom. Holds up well in the heat.*

### Givenchy

**(Christensen, introduced by Armstrong, 1985; 'Gingersnap' x 'Double Delight').** *High-centered, exhibition quality flowers in blends of pink, orange, yellow, and red. Often blooms in clusters. One of the most fragrant new roses. Medium height.*

### Sheer Bliss

**(Warriner, introduced by Jackson & Perkins, 1987; 'White Masterpiece' x 'Grand Masterpiece'; AARS 1987).** *Large, long, pointed, exhibition-quality buds open quickly to free-form flowers, blush colored with flesh-pink tones. Light tea fragrance. Very tall and vigorous bush. Good disease resistance.*

### Mikado

**(Suzuki, 1987; AARS 1988).** *High-centered, fire-red flowers with pointed petals, yellow at the base. Very fragrant. Stems too short and flowers too small to be exhibition quality. Outstanding color, especially during hot weather. Dark, glossy, disease-resistant foliage.*

### World Peace

**(Perry, introduced by Co-operative Rose Growers, 1989; 'First Prize' x 'Gold Glow').** *Large, long-stemmed, exhibition quality flowers in blends of red, yellow, and pink. Blooms best in cool weather. Resistant to disease and cold. Good cut flower.*

## Polyanthas

Jean-Baptiste Guillot, who is credited with the first hybrid tea, was also responsible for developing another class of roses, the polyanthas, which he introduced in the 1870s and 1880s. These were a cross between *R. multiflora* and a dwarf China rose. Polyanthas are low-growing shrubs with large clusters of small flowers (polyantha means "many flowered"). Because they generally grow only about two feet high, they make good bedding plants or low hedges. In the Cranford Rose Garden they are used as edging plants around the floribundas in the five central beds. They bloom continuously throughout the summer, and they are extremely hardy; but they have little scent. Polyanthas played an important role in the development of the floribundas.

At the beginning of the growing season, thin out polyanthas, removing old and dead wood, and cut them back lightly. If necessary, the larger-growing bushes can be pruned back by about two thirds. To get the best flower production, deadhead during the growing season. Polyanthas will do perfectly well if they are left on their own, however.

'Perle d'Or' and 'Marie Pavié' are two of the older polyanthas, once very popular as corsage or "sweetheart" roses. 'Clotilde Soupert', one of the earliest polyanthas on the market, was mentioned in 1894 as a superior rose in the White House rose garden.

'Tip-Top' was one of the original roses planted in the Cranford Rose Garden in 1927. It later went out of favor and was thought to be lost to cultivation, no longer growing even in the Cranford Garden, until a specimen was discovered in 1987 in a private garden in Shreveport, Louisiana. New plants were propagated from this for the Cranford Garden. (In the meantime, a floribunda raised by Tantau in 1963 had usurped its name.) 'Tip-Top' has long buds that were described in the 1923 Bobbink and Atkins catalogue as "*par excellence* for buttonholes."

### *Rosa wichuraiana*

**R. wichuraiana** is a creeping rose native to coastal regions of Japan, China, and Korea. Discovered in 1861 by the German botanist for whom it is named, Dr. Max Ernst Wichura, it was introduced to the United States through the Arnold Arboretum later in the nineteenth century. In this country R. wichuraiana, a popular ground cover, is often called the 'Memorial Rose' because it is used as a grave blanket. Some of the graves in the Friends' Cemetery in Prospect Park in Brooklyn are planted with specimens of this rose that were obtained from the Cranford Rose Garden.

R. wichuraiana has shiny leaves, deadly prickles, and small, white, very fragrant flowers. In the fall the leaves turn yellow and there are red hips. It has been used extensively by hybridizers in the United States to create hardy, disease-resistant climbers, and it has also played a part in the development of some of the polyanthas.

*Previous pages, left to right:* 'Night 'n' Day', 'Mary Lyons', 'World Peace', 'Redgold', 'Autumn Sunset'. *Right:* 'Orange Triumph', growing in classic polyantha form.

## Perle d'Or

**(Rambaud, introduced by Dubreuil, 1884; a polyantha x 'Mme. Falcot').** Similar to 'Cécile Brunner', one of the original "sweetheart" roses. Perfect buds open to reflexed, starburst form, coppery-apricot flowers with button eyes. Very fragrant.

## Marie Pavié

**(Allégatière, 1888).** One of the oldest polyanthas. Pale white flowers with deep pink centers borne in clusters throughout the season. Once very popular as a corsage or "sweetheart" rose. A low-growing thornless shrub. Long, pointed leaves. Very hardy. Constantly blooming. Makes an excellent low hedge.

## Clotilde Soupert

**(Soupert & Notting, 1890; 'Mignonette' x 'Mme. Damaizin').** Clusters of round buds, tinted red on the outer petals, open to very double, flat, white flowers with blush to deep pink centers. Buds will not open fully if the weather is damp or cool. Very fragrant. Classic old garden rose look. Canes have large, hooked prickles. Excellent bedding plant.

## Tip-Top

**(Lambert, 1909; 'Trier' x R. foetida bicolor seedling).** Long buds open to flowers with classic "sweetheart" rose form. Sixteen white petals, Tyrian purple at the edges, slightly yellow at the bases. The blooms, occurring singly or in clusters, open quickly. Not much fragrance. Small, compact bush with long, pointed foliage. Now rare.

## La Marne

**(Barbier, 1915; 'Mme. Norbert Levavasseur' x 'Comtesse du Cayla').** *A freely blooming bedding rose with two-inch flowers borne in large clusters. Cupped blooms, pink with large, blush white centers and about fifteen petals. Color darkens in cooler weather. Light fragrance. Bushy. About two feet high. A fine border plant that is never out of bloom.*

## Dick Koster

**(Koster, 1929; a sport of 'Anneke Koster').** *Clusters of small, one-inch, cup-shaped flowers with twenty to twenty-five deep pink to red petals. No fragrance. Flowering canes nearly thornless. Small peduncles. Stipules show multiflora characteristics. Good as a potted plant for forcing.*

## The Fairy

**(Bentall, 1932; 'Paul Crampel' x 'Lady Gay').** *Enormous clusters of thirty to forty small, double flowers that open deep pink and fade to blush. No fragrance. Blooms nonstop. Deadly hooked prickles on the canes. Shiny, pointed leaves. Procumbent growth habit. Excellent as a standard. Tends to attract spider mites. Very hardy.*

## Jean Mermoz

**(Chenault, introduced by Hémeray-Aubert, 1937; R. wichuraiana x a hybrid tea).** *Clusters of tight, round buds open to fully reflexed pink flowers, one inch across, quartered and full. Petals have light pink edges and dark pink centers, No fragrance. Low growing. Disease resistant. Constantly in bloom.*

## Floribundas

Floribunda (cluster-flowered) roses are the result of crossing polyanthas and hybrid teas. Much of the original work on floribundas was done by the Danish hybridizer D. T. Poulsen, who was attempting to raise roses that would flourish in the harsh winters and short growing seasons of Scandinavia. Poulsen introduced what is considered the first floribunda, 'Rödhätte', in 1912, and his sons Dines and Svend continued his work with this type of rose. These roses were officially recognized as a class around 1939–1940, when one of the first AARS winners was a floribunda called 'World's Fair'. This rose, which had been introduced from Germany under another name ('Minna Kordes'), was marketed at the 1939 World's Fair in New York by the American firm of Jackson and Perkins, which would soon become the world's largest rose grower.

Floribundas are large, shrubby roses with clustered flowers. They are quite hardy, and they make good bedding plants because they flower continuously all summer long. There are many early floribundas, as well as quite a few of the important roses that led to their development, growing in the five central beds of the Cranford Rose Garden.

At the beginning of the season, prune floribundas back by one-third to outward-facing buds. Clean out the centers, remove dead and cluttered canes, and shape the bushes to even heights in a bed. Unless they have weak growth and skimpy canes, prune floribundas more gently during the rest of the summer so they will quickly produce flowers on short stems and provide constant color in the garden throughout the season.

Only a few of the hundreds of varieties of floribundas that grow in the Cranford Rose Garden are pictured here.

'Rödhätte', whose name means 'Red Riding Hood', is a cross between a red polyantha and a red hybrid tea; it was originally sold as a polyantha or a hybrid polyantha. It is no longer available commercially. 'Kirsten Poulsen' and 'Else Poulsen' are other Poulsen roses that were important in establishing the floribunda class. 'Betty Prior', one of the most popular floribundas ever developed, and 'Smiles' are important early American floribundas. Both were introduced by Jackson and Perkins. 'Smiles' was the work of Dr. J. H. Nicolas, former director of research at Jackson and Perkins, who was responsible for naming this class of rose.

## Rosa multiflora

*R. multiflora* is the notorious rose that nurserymen used to tout as a wonderful "living fence." Native to Japan, Korea, and China, it was discovered in the early nineteenth century and came to the United States in 1875. It spreads rapidly, and once naturalized it is almost impossible to eradicate.

In spite of its faults, *R. multiflora* is a very beautiful and important wild rose. It has attractive red hips, and its clusters of profuse white flowers are a joy to see in the countryside in early summer as they scramble up trees and spill over the embankments of highways and railroad tracks. Modern roses are often budded to the rootstock of this robust rose. *R. multiflora* is also the parent of many present-day roses, as it has been used extensively by hybridizers in the creation of ramblers, polyanthas, and floribundas. One of its distinctive characteristics is the presence of feathery appendages on the stipules, and many of its descendants have this trait.

### *Rödhätte*

**(Poulsen, 1912; 'Mme. Norbert Levavasseur' x 'Richmond').** *A dwarf plant with large clusters of cupped, one-inch cherry-red flowers. Eight to ten petals with white at the bases. Very yellow stamens. Peduncles slightly bristly. No fragrance. Constantly in bloom. No longer available commercially.*

### *Kirsten Poulsen*

**(Poulsen, 1924; 'Orléans Rose' x 'Red Star').** *A vigorous, bushy, constantly blooming rose with clusters of cupped, bright scarlet flowers with five petals. Peduncles short and bristly. An important early floribunda.*

### *Else Poulsen*

**(Poulsen, 1924).** *Long-stemmed clusters of large, single, deep pink flowers. The thorny plant is tall and very bushy, similar to 'Betty Prior' but much thornier, especially on the new growth. A constant bloomer.*

### *Betty Prior*

**(Prior, 1935, introduced by Jackson & Perkins, 1938; 'Kirsten Poulsen' x unnamed seedling).** *Large clusters of five-petaled, dark carmine-pink flowers, slightly cupped, often as many as ten to a cluster. No fragrance. Long, red, bristly peduncles. Tall, wide bush. Extremely disease resistant and hardy. Constantly in bloom,*

### Smiles

(**Nicolas, introduced by Jackson & Perkins, 1937;** '*Echo*' x '*Rev. F. Page-Roberts*'). *Clustered, free-form flowers, salmon-pink, about two inches across. Stamens exposed. Sixteen to eighteen petals, lighter color toward the centers, becoming deeper magenta-pink as they age. Slight fragrance. Now rare.*

### Dagmar Späth and Lafayette

(**'Dagmar Späth': Wirtz & Eicke, introduced by Späth, 1936; a sport of 'Lafayette') ('Lafayette': Nonin, introduced by Dreer, 1924;** '*Rödhätte*' x '*Richmond*'). *Often seen on the same plant. Flowers of 'Dagmar Späth' pure white, sometimes with a blush edge; 'Lafayette', cherry-crimson. Low growing. Susceptible to mildew and blackspot. Now rare.*

### Summer Snow

(**C. H. Perkins, introduced by Jackson & Perkins, 1938; sport of 'Climbing Summer Snow'**). *Pure white, twelve-petaled flowers, very loose and open. Outer petals of buds sometimes touched with green. Not much fragrance. Practically thornless. A low-growing shrub that is constantly in bloom. Often sports to a pink form, or even back to the climbing version.*

### Dusky Maiden

(**Le Grice, 1947;** [ '*Daily Mail Scented Rose*' x '*Étoile de Holland*'] x '*Else Poulsen*'). *Single dark velvet blooms with prominent yellow stamens. Flowers up to four inches across, borne singly or in clusters. The slightly ruffled petals fade to scarlet. Light fragrance. Fairly disease resistant and vigorous. Constant bloom.*

## Creating New Roses

All of the many varieties of roses in the world today are descended from species roses, roses that occur naturally in the wild and grow true from seed. Roses that are not species roses are hybrids, either natural or man-made. Most hybrid roses have such complex family trees that their seeds, carrying the characteristics of many forebears, produce offspring different from the immediate parents.

To understand the hybridization process it is necessary to be familiar with the structure of a rose blossom (see drawing). All rose flowers contain both male and female organs. At the center of the flower are the pistils, the female organs. Surrounding the pistils are the stamens, the male organs, which produce the pollen. When the pollen grains are released, they adhere to a sticky coating on the tips (stigmas) of the pistils and then grow down the stems (styles) of the pistils to the ovary, where they develop into seeds.

The hybridizer interrupts a rose's natural process of self-reproduction and cross pollinates it with a rose of his choice. First the hybridizer must decide which varieties to cross in order to create a desirable new rose. Characteristics such as attractive foliage, fragrance, disease resistance, and winter hardiness are just as important as beautiful flowers.

A mature flower to be used as the male parent is selected, and its ripe pollen is collected. Then a bud that is to become the female parent is chosen. Just before this bud opens, the hybridizer, leaving the bud on the stem, carefully pulls off all of its petals. With a small scissors or tweezers, the hybridizer then carefully cuts or pulls off all the stamens, leaving the pistils intact. Now all that remains of the bud are its pistils, sepals, and undeveloped hip. It is covered with a small paper or plastic bag so that the pistils will not be fertilized accidentally by insect or wind-borne pollen.

After a day or so, the bag is removed. If the pistils are sticky on top they are ready to be fertilized, and the ripe pollen from the rose selected as the male parent is brushed over the stigmas. The pollinated bud is again covered to prevent any further pollination from outside sources. If the fertilization has been successful, the hip will be noticeably swollen after about a week. Within several months it will turn red, yellow, or orange, indicating that the seeds within are mature and ready to be planted. The following year they will have developed into mature plants, and the hybridizer can decide which, if any, of the new hybrid roses are worth saving. Many will be discarded.

*Opposite:* 'Golden Slippers'.

1. Young blossom.
2. Removing petals.
3. Plucking stamems.
4. Removing pistil.
5. Pressing stamens to pistil.
6. Fertilized hip. Only a small percentage of new hybrid roses will be worth saving; many will be discarded.

### Pink Rosette

**(Krebs, introduced by Howard & Smith, 1948).** *Clusters of very tight, long pink buds open to two-inch, cupped, soft pink flowers. Up to fifty petals. Slight fragrance. A compact bush. Foliage susceptible to disease.*

### Vogue

**(Boerner, introduced by Jackson & Perkins, 1951; 'Pinocchio' x 'Crimson Glory'; AARS 1952).** *Long, elegant buds, clustered or single, open to deep-coral flowers, about two inches across, with about twenty loosely arranged petals. Light fragrance. Slow to bloom in heat. More prone to disease than some other floribundas.*

### Baby Blaze

**(Kordes, introduced by Jackson & Perkins, 1954; 'World's Fair' x 'Hamburg').** *Large clusters of three-inch cupped, cherry-red flowers with exposed white "eyes". Thirty to thirty-five petals. Never needs to be deadheaded. Poor fragrance. A very vigorous and carefree shrub that starts blooming early in the season and never stops. Grows tall and wide. Makes a good hedge plant. Now rare.*

### Ruby Lips

**(Swim, introduced by Armstrong, 1958; 'World's Fair' x 'Pinocchio').** *Very bright, cardinal-red flowers, about one and one-half inches across, borne in clusters. About twenty petals, the outer ones so dark in autumn they look like velvet. Light fragrance. Low-growing bush with small hooked prickles. Disease-resistant foliage. A good edging plant. Slow to bloom in hot weather.*

## *Ivory Fashion*

**(Boerner, introduced by Jackson & Perkins, 1958; 'Sonata' x 'Fashion'; AARS, 1959).** *Clusters of long, creamy buds open to large, cupped, antique white flowers, about four and one-half inches across. Twenty petals. Fairly good foliage. Moderate height. Good edging plant.*

## *Golden Slippers*

**(Von Abrams, introduced by Peterson and Dering, 1961; 'Goldilocks' x unnamed seedling; AARS, 1962).** *Clusters of pointed buds on bristly peduncles open quickly to beautiful orange flowers. Twenty petals, yellow on the reverse. Light fragrance. The ideal floribunda. An excellent bedding plant with a compact, low growth habit.*

## *Corsage*

**(Belden, introduced by Wyant, 1965; 'Blanche Mallerin' x 'White Swan').** *Large clusters of globular, cupped blooms, about two inches across, white with blush pink. The thirty to thirty-five petals become more white as they open. Very fragrant. A tall-growing, spreading bush. Above average disease resistance. Constantly in bloom. Now rare.*

## *Apricot Nectar*

**(Boerner, introduced by Jackson & Perkins, 1965; unnamed seedling x 'Spartan'; AARS, 1966).** *Apricot-colored flowers, up to five inches across, born singly or in large clusters. Twenty-five to thirty slightly ruffled petals arranged in cup form. Tea fragrance. Large, bushy plant with large, dark, pointed leaves. A magnificent rose that is constantly in bloom*

### *Escapade*

**(Harkness, 1967; 'Pink Parfait' x 'Baby Faurax').** *Clustered flowers, magenta with white and yellow centers. Exposed stamens. Looks rather like a wild rose. Twelve or fifteen petals. Light tea fragrance. Peduncles covered with red bristles. Glossy, light green foliage. Extremely disease resistant. One of the first floribundas of the season to come into bloom. A good rose for constant color.*

### *Angel Face*

**(Swim and Weeks, introduced by Conard-Pyle, 1968; ['Circus' x 'Lavender Pinocchio'] x 'Sterling Silver'; AARS 1969).** *Exhibition-type pointed buds open to large, deep lavender flowers, three to four inches across. High, pointed centers. About thirty wavy petals. Very fragrant. Low growing. Always in bloom except during extremely hot weather.*

### *Gene Boerner*

**(Boerner, introduced by Jackson & Perkins, 1968; 'Ginger' x ['Ma Perkins' x 'Garnette Supreme'] AARS, 1969).** *Clusters of high-centered, deep pink flowers with exposed yellow stamens. More than thirty-five reflexed petals. Tea fragrance. Nearly thornless, bushy plant. Vigorous. Disease resistant. Constantly in bloom.*

### *Evening Star*

**(Warriner, introduced by Jackson & Perkins, 1974; 'White Masterpiece' x 'Saratoga').** *An outstanding white rose with three-to four-inch exhibition quality flowers often clustered on single, medium-length stems. Pointed, yellow-tinted centers. Tea fragrance. Foliage dark and disease resistant. Exceptional fall blooms.*

*Opposite:* 'Redgold'.

### Europeana

**(de Ruiter, 1963, introduced by Conard-Pyle, 1968; 'Ruth Leuwerik' x 'Rosemary Rose'; AARS 1968)** *Clusters of deep velvety red flowers with 25 to 30 petals. No fragrance. Bush moderately high. Disease-resistant foliage. Always in bloom. A wonderful bedding plant.*

### Montana

**(Tantau, 1974; 'Walzertraum'; x 'Europeana').** *Clusters of long, pointed buds open wide to fiery orange-red flowers, two to three inches in diameter. Twenty wavy petals, which do not reflex, become velvety red at the tips as they age. Lightly fragrant. Large, dark, glossy, pointed leaves. Constantly in bloom, even during a heat wave.*

### Summer Fashion

**(Warriner, introduced by Jackson & Perkins, 1985; 'Precilla' x 'Bridal Pink').** *Long, pointed buds, creamy white with rose-tinted margins, open to large, four-inch blooms that become more pink around the edges as they age. Flowers born singly or in clusters. About twenty-five petals. Tea fragrance. Low growing. Glossy, very disease-resistant foliage. Freely blooming.*

### Pleasure

**(Warriner, introduced by Jackson & Perkins, 1990; seedling of a hybrid tea x 'Intrigue'; AARS, 1990).** *Pink buds mottled with red open to large, short-stemmed, ruffled, shell-pink flowers with open centers. Four inches across. A good bedding plant with a moderate growth habit.*

*Opposite:* 'Lagerfeld'.

## Grandifloras

The first official grandiflora, a cross between a hybrid tea and a floribunda, was 'Queen Elizabeth', raised by the American hybridizer Dr. Walter E. Lammerts and introduced in the United States by Germain's Nursery of Los Angeles in 1954. 'Queen Elizabeth' was an All America Rose Selection in 1955, and it became one of the most popular roses of the twentieth century, winning many international gold medals.

The flowers of the original grandiflora are clustered, like the typical floribunda, but larger, and they have the long stems of the hybrid teas. Created as bedding plants, grandifloras grow very tall, often over six feet, and they are therefore useful at the back of the garden. They give good masses of color, blooming more frequently than the hybrid teas and opening quickly rather than holding perfect bud form. They are still flowering vigorously when the hybrid perpetuals and hybrid teas have slowed their bloom.

For the production of large flowers, grandifloras, like hybrid teas, need to be severely pruned. If they are used as background plants, however, prune them just to the desired height.

Many of the grandifloras in the Cranford Rose Garden grow in beds in front of the Rose Arc. All of those pictured here were created or introduced by Americans.

*Opposite:* 'Queen Elizabeth'. *Above:* 'Mount Shasta'.

## Lagerfeld

('Christensen, introduced by Armstrong, 1985; 'Blue
Nile' x ['Ivory Tower' x 'Angel Face']).

## June Bride

(Shepherd, introduced by Bosley Nursery, 1957;
['Madame Butterfly' x 'New Dawn';] x 'Crimson Glory').
Clustered, creamy buds, sometimes tinged with red, open to
fragrant, soft white flowers with about thirty petals. The
centers, high and pointed at first, later become cupped.
Upright and vigorous bush with crinkled, leathery foliage.
Vicious prickles. Now rare.

## Scarlet Knight

(Meilland, introduced by Conard-Pyle, 1967;
['Happiness' x 'Independence'] x 'Sutter's Gold'; AARS
1968). Rich black-red buds open to large, cupped fire-red
flowers, four to five inches across. Thirty-five to forty petals.
Light tea fragrance. Hardy bush with large, leathery leaves.
Very vigorous.

## Gold Medal

(Christensen, introduced by Armstrong, 1982; 'Yellow
Pages' x ['Granada' x 'Garden Party']). Buds open in
classic exhibition style to large, long-stemmed flowers, strong
deep yellow, often streaked with red and orange. Extremely
fragrant. Very vigorous and disease-resistant bush, over six
feet tall. One of the best yellow roses.

## Arizona

(Weeks, introduced by Conard-Pyle, 1975; [('Fred Howard' x 'Golden Scepter') x 'Golden Rapture'] x [('Fred Howard' x 'Golden Scepter') x 'Golden Rapture']; AARS 1975). Urn-shaped buds open to long-stemmed, high-centered, coppery orange flowers in blends of yellow and red. Very fragrant. Constant bloom. Susceptible to disease.

## Hotel Hershey

(J. B. Williams, introduced by Hershey Estates, 1977; 'Queen Elizabeth' x 'Comanche'). Pointed, urn-shaped buds open to high-centered, deep coral-orange flowers with ruffled petals. Thirty-five to forty ruffled petals. Light tea fragrance. Moderate growth habit and dark foliage.

## Sundowner

(McGredy IV, introduced by Edmunds, 1978; 'Bond Street' x 'Peer Gynt'; AARS 1979). Pointed buds open to large, double, golden orange flowers, about four inches across, with classic exhibition form. About thirty-five petals. Very fragrant. Tall, upright growth. Fairly good disease resistance.

## Mary Lyon

(Williams, introduced by Mt. Holyoke College, 1989; ['Mt. Shasta' x 'Sonia'] x ['White Masterpiece' x 'Ivory Fashion']).

## Shrub Roses

"Shrub rose" is a catchall term. In general, these are roses that have a robust, spreading growth habit and give fairly constant bloom. Some have single flowers, while others have very double, exhibition-type blooms. In this class one also finds hybrids that are closely linked to species roses, hybrids of climbers and bush-type roses, and anything hybridizers can't fit neatly into the category of hybrid tea, floribunda, or grandiflora. Most shrub roses can be used as landscape plants or trained as short climbers.

If shrub roses are grown as specimen (single) plants or as parts of high borders where they have to blend in with other bushes, prune them lightly to thin out the older wood and keep them from looking out of place. They can also be severely pruned back like grandifloras.

All the shrub roses pictured here were created or introduced by Americans. 'Autumn Bouquet' is one of the older varieties. Its flowers fill the air in the Cranford Rose Garden with a wonderful fragrance from the end of May into fall. 'Summer Wind' is a lesser-known creation of Griffith Buck, a pioneer in the rose world who is working to develop shrub roses that will survive Iowa winters and be beautiful as well. 'Sea Foam' is another extremely hardy variety. 'Belinda's Rose' is a compact, vigorous, disease-resistant shrub that looks very much like a hybrid perpetual. This new introduction does very well in Brooklyn, where it is constantly in bloom, but it grows even larger in hot, southern climates.

*Left:* 'Pike's Peak', a descendant of *Rosa acicularis*, a native North American rose.

### Autumn Bouquet

(Jacobus, introduced by Bobbink & Atkins, 1948; 'New Dawn' x 'Crimson Glory'). Very tight buds open to clustered carmine-pink flowers, up to three inches across, with tight, pointed centers. Petals slowly reflex. Wonderfully fragrant. Upright, contained bush with tough, leathery leaves and mean prickles. Now rare.

### Summer Wind

(Buck, introduced by Iowa State University, 1975; ['Fandango' x 'Florence Mary Morse'] x 'Applejack'). Large, carmine-pink flowers with exposed yellow stamens. Eight to ten slightly notched petals; those toward the inside have a faint white stripe down the center. Sweet scented. Vigorous and disease-resistant. Constantly in bloom.

### Sea Foam

(Schwartz, introduced by Conard-Pyle, 1964; [('White Dawn' x 'Pinocchio') x ('White Dawn' x 'Pinocchio')] x ['White Dawn' x 'Pinocchio']). Clusters of creamy white, double flowers. Light fragrance. Low-growing, spreading shrub with large, hooked prickles and small, glossy, disease-resistant leaves. Will grow anywhere. Can be trained as a climber. Carefree and constantly blooming.

### Belinda's Rose

(Basye, introduced by Antique Rose Emporium, 1989; 'Tiffany' x 'Jersey Beauty'). A beautiful new shrub rose that looks very much like a hybrid perpetual. Large, high-centered, exhibition style, shell-pink flowers, up to four inches in diameter. Short stems. Very fragrant. A vigorous and disease-resistant shrub with a compact growth habit. Constantly in bloom.

### Cinderella

(de Vink, introduced by Conard-Pyle, 1953; 'Cécile Brunner' x 'Tom Thumb'). *Also known as a micro-mini. Nine inches to one foot tall. Tiny, long-stemmed, perfectly formed blush-colored blooms, one-half inch in diameter. Long, pointed, disease-resistant leaves. Makes a good miniature hedge in the garden. Sometimes grows naturally into a mini-standard.*

### Red Cascade

(Moore, introduced by Sequoia Nursery, 1976; R. wichuraiana x 'Floradora'). *Long-stemmed, deep red flowers. Pointed petals have white at the bases. Climbing miniature, up to twenty feet in warm climates, three to four feet in cooler climates, where it makes a good ground cover. Looks well cascading down a wall. Blooms well even in partial shade. Very thorny.*

### Sweet Chariot

(Moore, introduced by Moore Rose Nursery, 1984; 'Little Chief' x 'Violette'). *Clustered, double, starburst shape, deep magenta flowers. More than forty petals with subtle white stripes down the centers. One of the most fragrant miniature roses. Upright bush grows two or two and one-half feet tall. Long, pointed, light green leaves. Better in cool than hot, dry weather. Grows very well in containers.*

### Mossy Gem

(Kelly, 1984; 'Heidi' x 'Violette'). *A modern moss rose in miniature. Flat, one-inch, bright magenta flowers on single stems. Pointed petals. Light fragrance. Mossy, reddish calyx. Its poor disease resistance does not affect its ability to bloom all season long.*

## Miniature Roses

The miniature is another rose whose origin remains a mystery. It supposedly goes back to *Rosa chinensis minima*, which was said to have been brought from either China or Mauritius to England in the early 1800s. No such rose has ever been discovered in China, however. The miniature rose was popular in nineteenth-century England, where it was called 'Miss Lawrance's Rose' after the popular flower painter Mary Lawrance (even though she probably never painted this rose), and 'Fairy Rose'. Later in the nineteenth century, the miniature lost its popularity and was practically forgotten until it turned up again during World War I, growing in a window box in Switzerland. Then it acquired a new name, *Rosa rouletii*, in honor of Dr. Roulet, the Swiss army surgeon who discovered it. A Swiss nurseryman obtained cuttings and propagated the rose, reintroducing it to the world in 1922. Hybridizers were quick to realize its possibilities, and soon there were many varieties on the market, including 'Tom Thumb', which was brought to this country from Holland by Robert Pyle of the Conard-Pyle company in 1936 and was the first miniature rose patented in the United States. In the past ten or fifteen years, miniatures have become extremely popular in the United States, primarily due to the work of Ralph Moore in California, and there are thousands of varieties on the market. Several other growers in the United States specialize in these roses; many miniatures developed by Americans grow in the Cranford Rose Garden.

With the exception of cascading and climbing types, miniature roses grow only ten to eighteen inches high, and they have proportionately small leaves, flowers, and stems. They are very popular for containers and window boxes. In gardens they can be planted by themselves or combined with larger shrubs. They are attractive when grown around standard roses or at the edges of beds. There are cascading, trailing, and climbing varieties — even micro-miniatures. All of them are very hardy. Unlike many modern roses that are budded (grafted to the rootstocks of other roses), most miniatures grow on their own roots.

Miniatures in the garden are pruned

'Beauty Secret'

differently from full-size roses. For the first few seasons, shear them back to the desired height, or to an even level if they are planted in a mass. Climbing varieties are simply tied in place. Twiggy growth should be thinned out regularly; growing close to the ground, these roses attract spider mites as they mature and fill out.

There are more than two hundred varieties of miniature roses in the Cranford Rose Garden. The four that are pictured here were all developed by American hybridizers. 'Cinderella', a direct descendant of 'Tom Thumb', grows from nine inches to one foot tall and has tiny leaves, flowers, and stems; it is called a micro-mini. Its long-stemmed, perfectly formed flowers are only one-half inch in diameter. 'Mossy Gem', one of the first roses to bloom in the garden, is a modern moss rose in miniature. 'Red Cascade' is a climbing mini that can grow up to fifteen or twenty feet tall in warm climates. In Brooklyn, where it reaches three to four feet, it grows well as a ground cover or cascading down a wall. At the moment, it covers an old tree stump. 'Sweet Chariot' is one of the most fragrant miniature roses.

*Top:* A display of miniature roses in the Cranford Rose Garden. Minis grown by themselves can make a beautiful garden. *Above:* 'New Beginning'. *Right:* A bouquet of miniature roses.

## *Oriental Simplex*

**(Williams, 1987).** *Dainty, five-petaled, half-inch flowers, fire orange with yellow centers. Looks like a miniature 'Austrian Copper'. Fairly long stems. Repeats well. Good disease resistance. Bush four inches high. A fine mini to use as a bedding plant.*

## *Lavender Jewel*

**(Moore, introduced by Sequoia Nurseries, 1978; 'Little Chief' x 'Angel Face').** *Double, lavender-mauve flowers with high centers and exhibition form. One inch across. Up to thirty-eight petals. Light fragrance. Always in bloom. Dense, bushy growth. A compact mini to grow as an edging plant or in pots.*

## *Arizona Sunset*

**(Jolly, introduced by Rosehill Farms, 1985; ['Orange Sweetheart' x 'Zinger'] x 'Party Girl').** *Light yellow flowers, cupped, about one inch across, with flushes of orange and red. Up to twenty petals. Faint fragrance. Slow to flower in heat. Low, spreading growth habit. A good bedding plant.*

## *Apricot Mist*

**(Saville, introduced by Nor'East, 1987).** *Double, one inch, exhibition form flowers on long stems. Lovely shades of apricot. Fragrant. Good repeat bloom. Excellent in mass plantings, in containers, and planted under standards.*

Training a climber.

## Climbing Roses

No roses are climbers in the sense that they have tendrils or other means with which to climb on their own; if not supported, they are just large shrubs that grow up and arch over. Some roses, however, have such long canes that they need to be supported, and these are called climbers. Climbing roses can be broken into two groups, climbers and ramblers.

Essentially, climbers have stiffer canes than ramblers. These canes grow either from older canes or from the base of the plant. Most climbers also develop laterals (side shoots off the canes) and produce flowers on them. Some varieties also bear flowers at the ends of the new canes. Certain climbers are everblooming, while others bloom only at the beginning of the season. A number of climbers are sports of hybrid teas and floribundas. These sports, which are not as hardy as the other climbers, perform best in warm climates; in colder northern regions, their flowering wood may die back in the winter.

Ramblers have smaller leaves and very flexible shoots that can grow quite long in one season. These supple shoots grow from the base of the plant each year and produce laterals that flower the following summer. The flowers are usually borne in clusters, and most of them do not repeat their bloom during the season. The majority of the ramblers are hybrids of *R. wichuraiana*. The first successful rambler, however, was a *R. multiflora* hybrid called 'Crimson Rambler'.

Some of the most important rose hybridizing in the United States has been done with climbing roses, by breeders seeking plants that can withstand the extreme climates of various

## Dr. Walter Van Fleet (1857-1922)

One of America's greatest early rose hybridizers worked in relative obscurity in the Bureau of Plant Industry at the Department of Agriculture. Dr. Walter Van Fleet was a medical doctor, but he gave this up because his real love was plant hybridization. He developed blight-resistant chestnuts and improved varieties of strawberries, gladioli, cannas, corn, gooseberries, and other plants. He also published several books on plant breeding. Today, however, he is best known for his wonderful climbing roses.

Van Fleet had definite ideas about what kinds of roses were needed for American gardens. Realizing that many of the new hybrid teas from England and Europe would not thrive in the colder areas of the United States without "incessant coddling," he worked to create varieties he called "dooryard roses": roses with beautiful flowers, luxuriant foliage, colorful hips, resistance to disease, and the ability to thrive in our country's harshest climates. To accomplish this, he crossed many types of roses with the newly discovered species roses from the Far East, developing hardy climbing roses that have become famous all over the world—'Silver Moon,' 'American Pillar', and 'Dr. W. Van Fleet' are only a few. A shy and modest man who disliked publicity, he did not want a rose named for him, but the nursery that introduced 'Dr. W. Van Fleet' prevailed.

When Van Fleet died suddenly in 1922, he left behind a great many seedlings of new roses. Others at the Department of Agriculture carried on his work, and some of his finest roses were made available years after his death. Specimens of two of them, 'Sarah Van Fleet' and 'Dr. E. M. Mills', were given to the Brooklyn Botanic Garden and became part of the original planting in the Cranford Rose Garden in 1927.

## New Dawn

**(Somerset Rose Nursery, introduced by Dreer, 1930; sport of 'Dr. W. Van Fleet').** *Blush-colored flowers borne singly or in clusters. Tea scented. Glossy, disease-resistant foliage turns yellow in the fall. Sets hips. Strong prickles. Can grow over ten feet in one year. Difficult to confine in a small garden. Repeats its bloom right into frost. Has given rise to many other new roses.*

## White Cap

**(Brownell, 1954; unnamed seedling x 'Climbing Break o'Day').** *Cupped and quartered flowers, borne singly or in clusters, almost pure white, sometimes with a hint of blush at the centers. Fifty to sixty petals. Fragrance of old garden roses. Grows about ten feet tall. Dark foliage and many hooked prickles. Absolutely carefree and hardy. Blooms nonstop all season. Now rare.*

## Cadenza

**(Armstrong, introduced by Armstrong Nurseries, 1967; 'New Dawn' x climbing 'Embers').** *Clusters of cup-shaped, deep velvet red flowers. Fragrant. Large hips. Exceptionally disease resistant. Deadly prickles. Extremely vigorous, often growing fifteen feet tall. Nonstop bloomer. No longer in commerce.*

## Golden Arctic

**(Brownell, 1954; unnamed seedling x 'Free Gold').** *Flat, very double, starlike, deep yellow flowers in clusters on single long stems. Blooms are three to four inches across and have more than forty petals. Extremely fragrant. Very vigorous and disease resistant. Strong red prickles. Light green foliage. A constant bloomer. Now rare.*

Climbers on metal arches over walkways in the Cranford Rose Garden. *Top:* 'Chevy Chase'.
*Right:* 'New Dawn'. *Above:* 'Shalom', a vigorous floribunda that is often trained on a low fence or pillar.

regions of the country. Most of our tough American climbers can be directly linked with *R. wichuraiana* and *R. multiflora*, extremely hardy wild roses from the Far East that can be considered climbers, and *R. setigera*, the native American species climber. In the early twentieth century, Dr. Walter Van Fleet did a great deal of work with *R. wichuraiana*. M. H. Walsh and Dr. and Mrs. Walter Brownell have also made very significant contributions to the development of climbing roses.

Climbers and ramblers can grow free, without support, but they are hard to contain. They are best trained on fences and walls and in fan shapes up the sides of houses. They can be wrapped in spiral fashion around pillars and posts, or trained over archways. It is important to remember that it is the arching habit of climbers and ramblers that causes them to produce abundant flowers. Bending the canes stimulates the production of hormones that spur growth of new laterals for flowers. Therefore, these roses should be trained so that as many canes as possible are parallel to the ground; this induces them to send out numerous laterals so they will flower luxuriantly from base to tip. In the Cranford Rose Garden, all the climbers and ramblers are wrapped around pillars and posts or trained in fan shapes.

Leave newly planted climbers alone for two seasons while they produce enough new canes for abundant blooms. Pruning is done after they have finished flowering. (For nonrepeating climbers, this is right after the blooming period.) If there are enough canes, remove one-third of them, and then follow each remaining cane from the base to the tip, locating all the laterals that produced flowers that season and shortening them by two-thirds. Some climbers repeat their bloom, and these receive their major pruning during their winter dormant period. Prune them in the same way as nonrepeating climbers. While they are flowering, however, simply shorten the laterals by deadheading them back by about two-thirds. 'New Dawn' and her offspring are exceptions to this rule: when deadheading them, simply remove the spent flowers to the first set of leaves, as the new growth is right behind the old.

Most ramblers bloom only once, some at the beginning of the season, others in midsummer.

Since they bloom best on the previous year's wood, cut the wood that has borne flowers down to the ground so that many supple new canes will come up and produce flowers the following year.

Some ramblers produce only a few new canes from the base, bearing the majority of their new canes on old wood. If this is the case, remove some of the old wood to stimulate new growth, but leave much of it, especially if the plant is growing in an area where it can spread out and grow naturally. In formal gardens like the Cranford Rose Garden, where ramblers must be kept neat and tidy, they are all pruned carefully each year down to three or four canes and trained on arches, pillars, and lattices.

Unfortunately, ramblers, especially 'Dorothy Perkins' and 'Excelsa', are very susceptible to diseases and spider mites. For this reason it is important to cut out as many of the old canes as possible; this allows for good air circulation and prevents cluttering.

Many important ramblers and climbers have been developed in the United States. All those pictured here are the work of Americans or have American roses in their heritage. Climbers and ramblers cover all the pillars, pergolas, arches, and latticework in the Cranford Garden.

'New Dawn', the first plant to be patented, is a wonderful climber with all the good qualities of its parent, 'Dr. W. Van Fleet', plus the ability to repeat its bloom right into frost. It has given rise to many other new roses. 'Cadenza' is no longer in commerce, which is unfortunate as this is one of the best red climbers ever created. 'Golden Arctic' is a climber with flowers that are almost starlike, a characteristic of many Brownell roses.

'Dorothy Perkins' is a very popular rambler named for the granddaughter of the founder of the Jackson and Perkins Company. It has produced many important sports. 'Excelsa', with its hanging clusters of bright red flowers, is a rambler that looks wonderful no matter where it is grown. This very thorny rose, which has glossy foliage, produces new ten- to thirteen-foot canes each season; these are very pliable and can be trained over fences and walls. 'Excelsa' is also beautiful growing wild or climbing into trees.

## America

**(Warriner, introduced by Jackson & Perkins, 1976; 'Fragrant Cloud' x 'Tradition'; AARS 1976).** *Pointed buds open to vibrant, pure salmon-pink flowers, about three inches across. Light fragrance. Repeats throughout the summer. Good disease resistance. Not a vigorous climber, reaches only about six feet.*

## Lawrence Johnston

**(Ducher, 1923; 'Mme Eugene Verdier' x R. foetida persiana).** *Clusters of large, semidouble, solid yellow flowers, up to five inches across. Fragrant. Repeats its bloom. One of the earliest yellow climbers, can reach thirty feet. Suffers winter dieback in cold climates. Susceptible to blackspot.*

## Piñata

**(Suzuki, introduced by Jackson & Perkins, 1978).** *Clusters of four to five urn-shaped buds open to multi colored yellow-blend flowers with up to twenty-eight petals. Flowers turn from yellow to vivid scarlet as they age. Slow-growing climber. Blooms best in cool weather, and prefers partial shade. Susceptible to frost dieback.*

## Altissimo

**(Delbard-Chabert, introduced by Cuthbert, 1966; 'Tenor' x unknown).** *Large, cupped to flat blood-red flowers with seven petals. Clove fragrance. Vigorous climber that can grow ten to twelve feet in one season. Flowers only at ends of canes unless canes are trained horizontally. Blooms constantly, even in partial shade. A good cut flower.*

## Dorothy Perkins

**(Jackson & Perkins, 1901;** R. wichuraiana x *'Mme. Gabriel Luizet')*. *Clusters of double, rose-pink flowers. Seldom reblooms. Little fragrance. Dark, glossy foliage. Threatening prickles. Susceptible to disease and insect problems. Has produced many important sports. Very popular.*

## Excelsa

**(Walsh, 1909;** R. wichuraiana x *a polyantha)*. *Hanging clusters of bright red flowers fade to a lighter red as they age. Does not repeat its bloom. No fragrance. Glossy foliage. Very thorny. Tends to suffer from mites and diseases. Pliable ten-to thirteen-foot canes can be trained over fences and walls.*

## Ivy Alice

**(Letts, 1927;** *a sport of 'Excelsa')*. *Flowers soft pink and salmon, tinged with carmine when fading. Light green foliage. Growth habit like 'Excelsa', but somewhat woodier. Now rare.*

## Chevy Chase

**(Hansen, introduced by Bobbink & Atkins, 1939; Rosa soulieana x *'Eblouissant')*. *Massive erect clusters of strong red flowers. No fragrance. Grayish green foliage. Canes heavily armed with strong, straight prickles. Can grow up to fifteen feet in one season. Extremely vigorous, hardy, and disease resistant. Does not repeat its bloom.*

'Ballerina', a vigorous hybrid musk.

## Hybrid Musk Roses

Hybrid musk roses, which were developed in England early in the twentieth century, are only remotely related to *R. moschata*, the Musk Rose. They were called musk roses by the Reverend Joseph Pemberton, who did extensive work with them, crossing two early ramblers that have distant hybrid musk influence ('Aglaia' and 'Trier', a seedling of 'Aglaia'), with teas, hybrid teas, and Chinas.

Hybrid musks are really "shrub" roses that can tolerate difficult growing conditions, such as poor soil and shade. Some of them set good hips. They can be grown as freestanding shrubs or trained as climbers. If they are grown as climbers, the laterals should be pruned back after the first flush of growth. Otherwise, removal of old wood is all that is necessary. Hybrid musks repeat their bloom, so they can be deadheaded to promote the best new flower production.

'Bloomfield Dainty' makes a good climber or pillar rose, but its canes become stiff as they age and should be trained while they are still young and flexible. 'Clytemnestra' is one of Rev. Pemberton's creations. It tends to grow in a procumbent fashion, and it can be trained on a pillar. It looks marvelous cascading near water, which is why Harold Caparn, the designer of the Cranford Rose Garden, had concentric rows of this rose planted around the pool in the Rose Arc area.

## Clytemnestra

**(Pemberton, 1915; 'Trier' x 'Liberty').** *Clusters of ten to twelve small, apricot-blend flowers. Eighteen to twenty ruffled, fully reflexed petals. Fragrant. Flowers at ends of long canes produce masses of color in June and repeat intermittently until first frost. Good disease resistance. Procumbent. Can be trained on a pillar.*

## Bloomfield Dainty

**(Thomas, introduced by Bobbink & Atkins, 1924; 'Danäe' x 'Mme. Edouard Herriot').** *Large, single, yellow flowers, up to three inches in diameter. Blooms fade to white as they age. Only a few repeats. Light fragrance. Canes have a few large, hooked prickles. Foliage not very disease resistant; bush tends to look bare by fall. Good climber or pillar rose.*

## Felicia

**(Pemberton, 1928; 'Trier' x 'Ophelia').** *Recurring clusters of semidouble, flat, pink flowers, slightly cupped and ruffled. Exposed stamens. Outer petals blush pink, inner petals a deeper pink. Hint of yellow at the base of the petals. Fragrant. Dark foliage. Few prickles. Vigorous. Good pillar specimen.*

## Will Scarlet

**(Hilling, 1948, introduced by Wayside Gardens, 1956; a sport of 'Skyrocket', which is also known as 'Wilhelm').** *Clusters of four to six scarlet-red flowers at ends of the canes. Twelve to sixteen petals, at least one of which has a white stripe down the center. Spicy fragrance. Large shrub, six feet high and wide. Blooms throughout the season.*

# 4 A Rose for Every

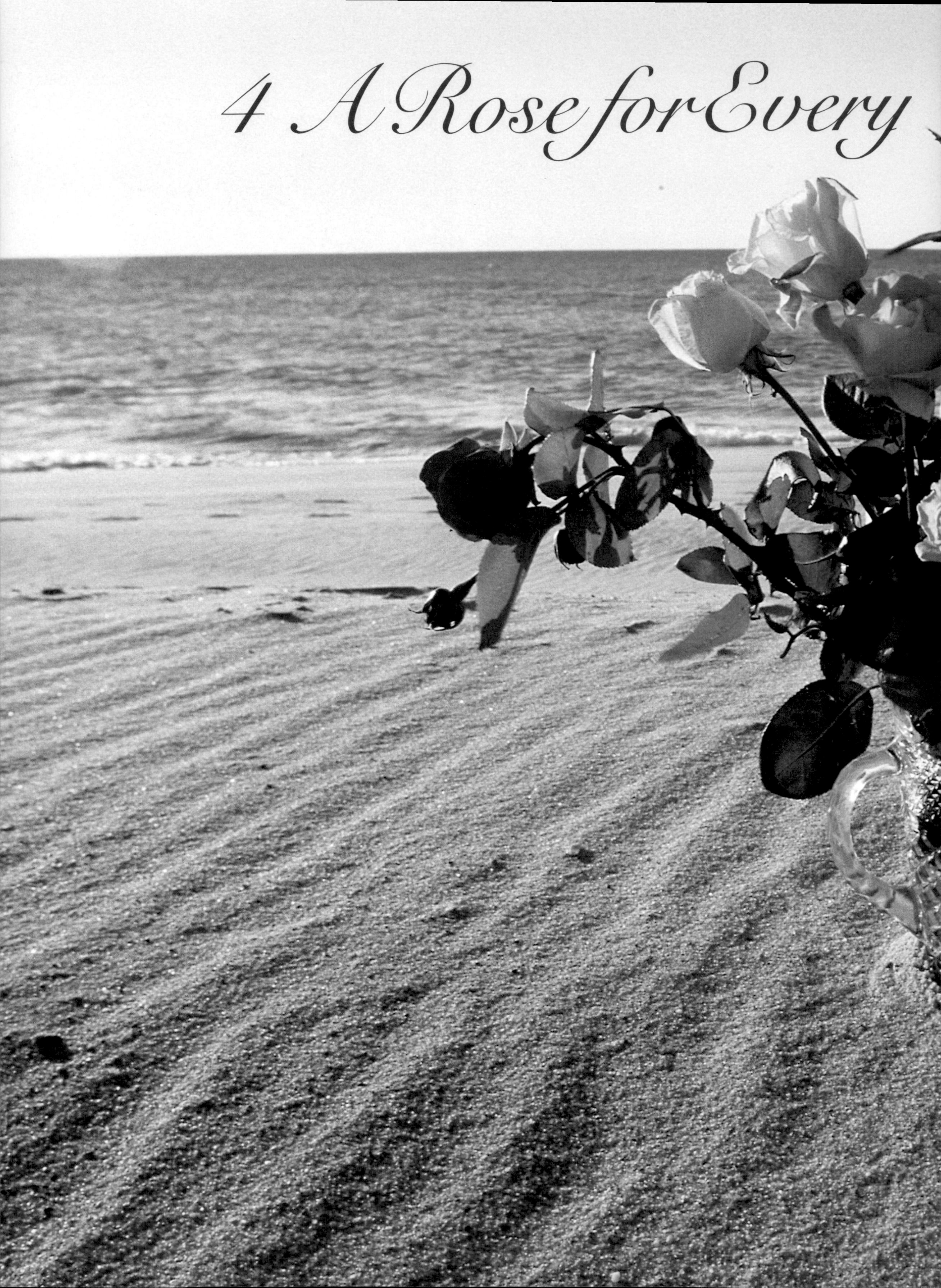

Landscape

## 4

# A Rose for Every Landscape

ince the days of Dr. Van Fleet, American hybridizers have been attempting to develop roses that will be hardy in all the varied climates and soils of the United States. This is a difficult task. In the mountains of Massachusetts, where old garden roses thrive, modern roses will not live through the winters without heavy protection. In the high altitude of Denver, climbing roses have to be released from their supports each winter and carefully wrapped and protected from cold, dry winds. In the extreme northern parts of North Dakota, the only roses that thrive without careful cold-weather protection are some species roses, exceptionally hardy shrub roses, and rugosa hybrids. During winter months in Iowa and Minnesota, gardeners must completely enclose most types of roses in ventilated boxes built over the beds.

In regions with winters that have prolonged periods of temperatures below 20 degrees Fahrenheit, teas, Chinas, Noisettes, Bourbons, and many modern roses suffer without winter protection because they start to grow during intervals of warm weather and then die when their tender new shoots are frozen during returning cold spells. In addition, alternating periods of freezing and thawing cause their roots to be heaved above the ground, where they freeze. Species roses, pre-China old garden roses, and hybrid teas, on the other hand, need a season of dormancy that nature does not provide in southern regions. In December, 'Electron', 'Betty Prior', and 'New Dawn' are dormant in New Hampshire, but in southern California they are growing and blooming, and they will wear themselves out unless gardeners force them to rest by stripping them of their foliage and pruning them back.

To make the problem even more complex, there are many micro-climates within each of the hardiness zones of the United States. For example, roses that do well in Brooklyn may not survive winters in other regions close by. 'Silver Moon', an extremely hardy and rampant Van Fleet climber that does not suffer winter damage in the Cranford Rose Garden, dies back during cold weather only one hundred miles north in the hills of Dutchess County, New York.

*Opposite:* This lavish garden was created in a normal-sized backyard. It shows what can be accomplished with creativity, hard work, and knowledge about roses.

*R. multiflora*

*R.* × *pteragonis*

*R. setigera*

*R. spinosissima altaica*

'La Belle Sultane'

'Common Red Moss'

When planning a rose garden, consider the fact that some roses have distinctive foliage. The examples on the opposite page show a variety of possibilities. *Above:* 'Spartan', a floribunda, tends to look naked at the end of the season. *Right:* By combining 'Spartan' with other roses, such as albas and damasks, you can create a screen to cover bare spots. *Following pages:* Roses come in many shapes, sizes, and colors.

Soils also differ in various parts of the country. The soil of coastal regions is loose and sandy; that of mountain localities may be full of rocks and pebbles. In New York City and surrounding counties, soils are acid; in the Rocky mountains, they are alkaline. Particularly difficult growing conditions are found in areas around Houston, Texas, which have heavy, black, slightly alkaline soil known locally as "gumbo." Roses will not thrive there unless they are planted in raised beds or in garden soil enriched with organic material and extra nitrogen.

The perfect rose for all regions of the United States has so far eluded hybridizers. Fortunately, there are many varieties, both old and modern, to choose from if you want to create a rose garden, no matter where you live. Success with roses depends on matching the variety with the climate. Species roses can be found for all climates and soils. The pre-China old garden roses thrive with almost no care in the north. The Chinas and China-influenced old garden roses perform well in warm, southern climates, where they need very little attention, even in the heat and droughts of arid regions. Most modern roses, desirable in gardens because they bloom through-

out the season, can be grown anywhere in the United States if they are given adequate winter protection. They simply require more work than the old roses.

Harold Caparn designed the Cranford Rose Garden as a garden where Americans could see that all types of roses will grow in this country. He knew that for many people the word "rose" meant hybrid tea because that was what they saw in flower shops and catalogues of the day. But he was also well aware that hybrid teas were not the best choices for all growing situations in the United States and that people from some regions of the country would become discouraged if they tried to design rose gardens filled with these modern roses. By including hundreds of varieties of species and old garden roses, which provide so many different colors, shapes, sizes, types of foliage, and growth habits that they can satisfy anyone's appetite for roses, he made the Cranford Rose Garden an inspiration for gardeners everywhere.

No matter where you live, you can grow numerous kinds of roses. The first step in designing a garden of these wonderful flowers is to decide how you want to use your roses. If you like

'Stanwell Perpetual', hybrid spinossisima

'Pink Rosette', floribunda

'Perle d'Or', polyantha

'World Peace', hybrid tea

'Poulsen's Pearl', floribunda

'Summer Snow', polyantha

'Old Blush', china

'Mervielles des Rouge', polyantha

'La Marne', polyantha

'Arizona Sunset', miniature

'Cadenza', climber

*Above:* 'Zephirine Drouhin' is a luxuriant Bourbon rose that can be trained as a climber. Here it is shown growing in Texas, where it flowers throughout the season. In the colder Northeast it will not repeat its bloom.

cut roses throughout the season, select the constantly blooming, long-stemmed varieties of hybrid teas and grandifloras. For good bedding effects, grow floribundas, polyanthas, miniatures, Chinas, and teas. For scent and potpourri, choose the sweet-smelling old garden roses — albas, damasks, centifolias, and hybrid perpetuals — and the most fragrant modern roses, such as the hybrid teas 'Jadis' or 'Curly Pink'. Also think about how much time you plan to spend maintaining your garden. The modern roses, which need winter protection in the north and require a great deal of pruning, will be more work than the species and old garden roses.

In general, roses with growth habits suitable for the main part of a garden are hybrid teas, floribundas, grandifloras, shrub roses, teas, Chinas, Bourbons, moss roses, gallicas, damasks, damask perpetuals, hybrid perpetuals, centifolias, and certain albas. The old garden roses listed in this group are not very tall, but they command more space than the modern roses because they have spreading growth habits, and they fall over when they are laden with flowers. For a low front border, use polyanthas, miniatures, and low-growing floribundas. Albas, damasks, rugosa hybrids, and most species roses have large growth habits or sucker freely and are therefore good freestanding background plants, hedges, and screens. Climbers, ramblers, Noisettes, and hybrid musks can be trained on pergolas, fences, walls, and pillars, or festooned on chains. Remember, however, that the growth habits of individual

rose varieties may vary from one part of the country to another. Tea roses, for example, which are spindly in the Northeast, grow into magnificent landscape shrubs in Texas, where they are often used as hedges. Many varieties of hybrid teas, which have sparse foliage in northern regions, grow into large, massive bushes in warmer climates. Visit your local botanical garden and study the growth habits of roses in your area.

The central part of the Cranford Garden is a formal rose garden consisting of symmetrical beds of roses surrounded by lawns. These beds are rectangular, but circular, square, or curved beds are also common in this type of garden. Rows of curving beds are often arranged in concentric patterns. If you are making a formal rose garden, remember to keep the beds a manageable size so you can work the soil without having to walk into them. Three feet is a suitable width for a bed open on one side; six feet for a bed that can be approached from both sides.

Modern roses are pleasing in formal gardens because when planted together in rows similar varieties of these roses are of uniform height. A rose garden should consist of more than static rows of beds where roses are displayed for their flowers, however. Take into consideration growth habits as well as flowers, and use different types of roses to create variations in height, width, and texture, contrasts of light and shade, and patterns of color. It is particularly difficult to create a successful rose garden using only hybrid teas: these roses have spectacular blooms, but their growth habit is stiff and upright, and their foliage tends to become sparse as the season progresses. Combine hybrid teas with other kinds of roses. Use, for example, taller-growing hybrid teas and grandifloras in the center of a bed edged with low-growing floribundas or polyanthas. Miniatures, which look well massed together, also make good edging plants. Climbing roses trained on pillars or, as in the Cranford Garden, festooned on chains or ropes, add height to formal beds. In areas of the country where they are winter hardy, standard (tree) roses also provide height. Other kinds of plants that can be pruned into uniform shapes, such as boxwood, yew, cedar, and holly, can be used to good effect in formal rose gardens.

*Opposite:* Use available structures when you plan your garden.

Arches, trellises, low stone benches, and flower pots can all be incorporated into your garden. When selecting roses, consider the fact that some varieties, such as *R. multiflora* (opposite above right) bear hips that are pleasing through the fall.

In the Cranford Rose Garden, species and old garden roses grow in beds around the perimeter, where their carefree growth habits contrast with the uniform qualities of the modern varieties in the central, formal part of the garden. The old roses enliven the garden with multi-textured foliage that turns red, yellow, and orange in the fall, and many of these roses have brilliant red and orange hips, distinctive prickles, and brightly colored canes that stand out in winter. In an informal garden—a cottage garden, for example—species and old garden roses can be used alone or combined with modern roses, such as hybrid teas and floribundas, as well as with constantly blooming perennials and herbs. Plants that have silver-gray foliage—such as lamb's-ears, artemisias, santolina, and certain sages—make excellent companions for old garden roses, as do plants with blue flowers, like lavender. Some shallow-rooted annuals, alyssum and lobelia, for example, make attractive ground covers that also help keep the roots of roses cool.

For cottage gardens in the north, pre-China old garden roses, species roses, and hybrid perpetuals are appropriate. Some modern climbing roses like 'New Dawn' can be added in the background. In hotter regions, such as southern California or Texas, teas and Chinas are suitable for cottage gardens; roses that have tall growth habits in warm climates—Noisettes, hybrid musks, and even some Chinas—can be substituted for climbers.

Roses can be incorporated into many types of flower gardens. Floribundas like 'Betty Prior' blend in well with tall-growing perennials and annuals. Miniatures are also good additions to a flower bed, either in the main section or around the edges. Old garden roses are charming companions for perennials; in fact, they are more attractive combined with these than planted in masses by themselves. Hybrid perpetuals, many of which have very long canes, can be trained horizontally on wires to make unique borders for some types of gardens. When planting roses with annuals and perennials, allow six inches between the main cane of each rose and the companion plant, and avoid combining roses with deep-rooted plants that compete for nourishment.

Climbing roses are versatile in many situations. In formal gardens they can be trained on pillars and posts to give height. On pavilions, lattices, and the sides of buildings, they have a more carefree, spreading form. On walls they are often grown with ivy, which hides their bare canes in winter. Left on their own, climbing roses can

cover banks, spill over walls and fences, or ramble up through the branches of trees.

Many roses, particularly species roses, old garden roses, and rugosa hybrids, thrive in the sandy soil and cool, moist air of coastal areas. *R. carolina* and *R. rugosa*, for example, have become naturalized in sand dunes all along the eastern seaboard. All modern and old garden roses make delightful seaside plantings, provided they are protected from strong winds by walls or hedges and their soil is supplemented with organic material. In cool, damp, foggy areas, such as the Pacific Northwest, northern California, and the eastern seaboard, avoid using many-petaled roses

This rose garden, created around a swimming pool, takes advantage of a lovely wooded setting.

Private gardens may be luxurious and formal or small and modest.

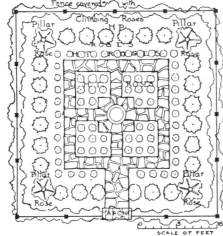

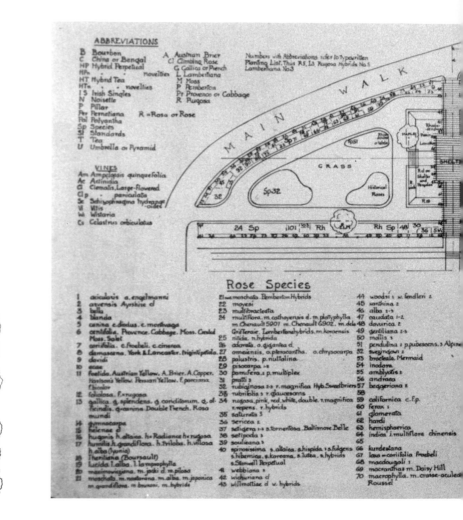

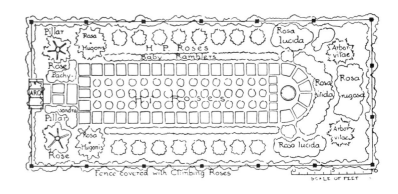

Garden plans by Harold Caparn, who believed that species and old garden roses should be used as frames for modern varieties. *Above:* An oblong arrangement. *Top:* Plans for the Cranford Rose Garden. *Left:* Design for a municipal rose garden. *Top left:* a rose garden created for a private estate.

ESPLANADE

TYPICAL

BEDS

GRASS

GRAVEL WALK

BANK

E. OF SCHWERDLER MAPLES

BROOKLYN BOTANIC GARDEN
ROSE GARDEN PLANTING DETAILS
July 30, 1927  TN5758 RG  Harold A. Caparn, Landscape
Scale, 16ft = 1 in.      New York      Architect

because their flowers ball up in wet weather.

As demonstrated in the Cranford Garden in Brooklyn, roses, which tolerate polluted conditions, are ideal for city gardens. In an urban backyard with trees, choose species and old garden roses because they bloom early in the season, before the trees leaf out and block the sun. Climbers, which grow up toward the light, can be used in shaded areas. On balconies and around penthouses, all kinds of roses can be grown in containers. Give them good soil, protection from the wind, and plenty of water so the sun does not dry them out. Modern roses, particularly miniatures and floribundas, will give constant color in these situations all summer long. Climbers can be trained along railings and over walls. Even tea roses can be grown successfully in the warm micro-climates of some northern cities.

When designing a rose garden, consider the enchanting effect of roses reflected in water, as in the Rose Arc at the Cranford Garden, where hybrid musks are mirrored in a pool. *R. wichurai-ana* is another rose that is especially attractive cascading by water.

When space allows, roses can be used in open landscape plantings. At the Brooklyn Botanic Garden, climbers, ramblers, species, and modern shrub roses wander up a hill from the Cranford Rose Garden to The Overlook. These varieties of roses can be planted in wild gardens, at the edges of fields or woodlands, and along highways and railway embankments. They bring beauty to many otherwise barren areas, yet they require no care, and their roots hold the soil. Species roses are especially well suited to naturalizing, and there is no better way to grow the lovely wild roses native to your area.

Although the ideal rose for all growing situations in the United States has yet to be developed, this should not deter anyone from cultivating these beautiful flowers. Even weekend gardeners who want to grow roses with a minimum of effort have hundreds of varieties to choose from. There is a rose for every landscape.

Roses can flourish even in the middle of a polluted city like New York. *Top:* An inner-city vest-pocket rose garden. *Above left:* The rose garden at the United Nations. *Above right:* A tiny backyard garden, newly planted with miniatures. *Right:* An indoor garden under lights in a window. *Opposite:* The Rockefeller Center rose garden.

# New Plant Hardiness — Zone Map

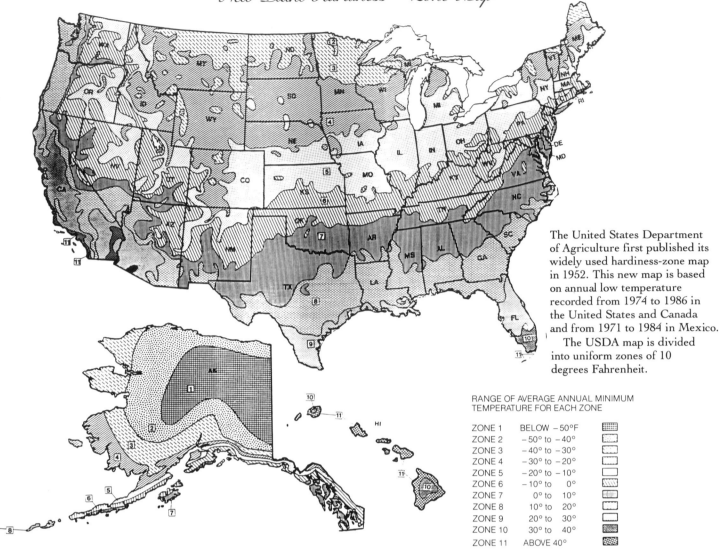

The United States Department of Agriculture first published its widely used hardiness-zone map in 1952. This new map is based on annual low temperature recorded from 1974 to 1986 in the United States and Canada and from 1971 to 1984 in Mexico.

The USDA map is divided into uniform zones of 10 degrees Fahrenheit.

RANGE OF AVERAGE ANNUAL MINIMUM
TEMPERATURE FOR EACH ZONE

| | |
|---|---|
| ZONE 1 | BELOW −50°F |
| ZONE 2 | −50° to −40° |
| ZONE 3 | −40° to −30° |
| ZONE 4 | −30° to −20° |
| ZONE 5 | −20° to −10° |
| ZONE 6 | −10° to 0° |
| ZONE 7 | 0° to 10° |
| ZONE 8 | 10° to 20° |
| ZONE 9 | 20° to 30° |
| ZONE 10 | 30° to 40° |
| ZONE 11 | ABOVE 40° |

## Schedule for Planting Bare Root Roses

| | JAN | FEB | MAR | APR | MAY | JUN | JUL | AUG | SEPT | OCT | NOV | DEC |
|---|---|---|---|---|---|---|---|---|---|---|---|---|
| Pacific Northwest | Plant | Plant | Plant | Plant | | | | | | | | |
| Pacific Seaboard | Plant | Plant | | | | | | | | | | |
| Southwest | Plant | | | | | | | | | | | Plant |
| South Central | Plant | Plant | | | | | | | | | | Plant |
| Mid South | | Plant | Plant | | | | | | | | Plant | |
| Subtropical | Plant | | | | | | | | | | | Plant |
| North Central | | | | Plant | Plant | | | | | Plant | Plant | |
| Eastern Seaboard | | | Plant | Plant | Plant | | | | | Plant | Plant | |
| Northeast | | | Plant | Plant | Plant | | | | | Plant | Plant | |

## Suitability Chart

Although there are roses in most groups that will thrive in any of the following situations or conditions, the ones marked with an "X" are highly recommended for exceptional bloom and/or carefree maintenance.

| | Species | Gallicas | Damasks | Albas | Centifolias | Moss | China | Tea | Bourbon | Noisette | Damask Perpetual | Hybrid Perpetual | Hybrid Tea | Polyantha | Floribunda | Grandiflora | Climber | Rambler | Miniature | Hybrid Musk | Shrub |
|---|---|---|---|---|---|---|---|---|---|---|---|---|---|---|---|---|---|---|---|---|---|
| Good Landscape Form | X | LTD | | X | | | X WC | X WC | X WC | X | X | | X | X | X | | X | X | | X | X |
| Edging Beds | | | | | | | | | | | X | | X | X | | | | | X | | |
| Hedge | X | X | | X | | | X WC | X WC | | | X | X | X | X | X | X | X | X | X | X | X |
| Fragrant Foliage | X | X | | | X | X | | | | | X | | | | | | | | | | |
| Screening | X | | | X | | | | | | | | | | | | X | X | X | | | X |
| Pillars | X | | X | X | X | X | | | X | X | X | X | | | | | X | X | | X | X |
| Hips | X | | LTD. | | | | X | | LTD. | | | | | | | | X | X | | X | X |
| Covering Fence | X | | X | X | LTD. | | | | X | X | X | X | | | | | X | X | | X | X |
| Foliage | X | X | | X | | | | | | | | | | | | | | | | | |
| Foggy-Misty Cool-Damp | X | SP | SP | | | | X | X | | X | SP | | | SP | | | X | X | X | X | SP |
| Dry-Arid | LTD | | X | X | X | | X | X | X | X | | | X | X | X | X | X | X | X | X | X |
| High Heat | LTD | | | | | | X | X | X | Y | X | X | X | X | X | X | X | X | X | X | X |
| High Altitude | X | X | X | X | X | X | | | | | | | | | | | | | | X | |
| Sandy Coast | X | X | X | X | X | X | X | X | | | | | X | X | | | X | X | X | X | X |

LTD: Limited
SP: Single-petal
WC: Warm Climate

## Schedule for Pruning Roses

| | JAN | FEB | MAR | APR | MAY | JUN | JUL | AUG | SEPT | OCT | NOV | DEC |
|---|---|---|---|---|---|---|---|---|---|---|---|---|
| Pacific Northwest | Prune | | | | | | | | | | | |
| Pacific Seaboard | | | | | | | | | | | | Prune |
| Southwest | Prune | | | | | | | | | | | |
| South Central | Prune | | | | | | | | | | | |
| Mid South | Prune | Prune | | | | | | | | | | |
| Subtropical | Prune | | | | | | | | | | | Prune |
| North Central | | | Prune | | | | | | | | | |
| Eastern Seaboard | | | Prune | | | | | | | | | |
| Northeast | | | Prune | Prune | | | | | | | | |

This chart applies to all modern roses except climbers and ramblers.

5 Growing Roses

CHAPTER

*5*

*Growing Roses*

## *Selecting Roses for the Garden*

here are no mysteries involved in successful rose growing—just a few simple rules anyone can follow. The first step is to buy strong, healthy plants from a reputable source. For those who are new to the world of roses, a local nursery is a good place to start. But even beginners will soon want to sample the larger selection available from mail-order nurseries. Winter is the time to study catalogues and become familiar with some of the thousands of varieties of roses on the market today.

Nurseries sell roses by grades: 1, 1½, and 2. Grades are a measure of quality. Roses classified as grade 1, which have at least three or four canes, are the best to start with. Grades 1½ and 2, which have fewer canes, will be less expensive, but they will need more care if they are to develop into top-quality plants. Whenever possible, order grade 1 roses, and check them carefully when they arrive to be sure the nursery sent what you ordered.

Some people believe they should buy roses only from nurseries located in parts of the country with climates similar to their own, but this is a myth; roses suitable for a particular climate will adjust to any area with that climate, no matter where they were originally grown. Most nurseries will send the plants at the appropriate time for planting in your region.

Roses are shipped dormant and bare rooted. Usually their roots and canes are wrapped in protective material, such as wet sphagnum moss. Plant them as soon as you receive them. If they arrive too late in the season for planting, you can keep them over the winter by heeling them into the garden or storing them in a cool place. Bare root roses can be planted in the spring or fall; in the Cranford Rose Garden, fall is preferred.

Local nurseries obtain their roses bare rooted in midwinter, pot them up, and sell them when they have leaves and possibly flowers. These containerized roses can be planted any time the ground isn't frozen, but they will take longer than bare root roses to become permanently established in the garden; having been confined to the pot, their roots need time to adjust and spread out.

*Opposite:* An example of a bare root grade #1 rose bush.

buds

prickles

canes

bud union

roots-rootstock

## Picking a Site

With the exception of the species roses, which have been around for so long that they can grow almost anywhere, roses need at least five hours of sunlight a day, ample water, and fertile, well-drained soil in a spot away from large trees and shrubs, whose roots would compete for nutrients and water. Good air circulation is essential so their leaves always have a chance to dry out during the day or after rain. The soil should be easily workable to the depth of about twenty-four inches. If not, use beds raised two feet above ground level. Roses do well in containers, but these must have good drainage and be large enough to allow for complete root development—no smaller than twenty-four inches for large bushes and climbers, and six inches for miniatures.

When choosing a site for a new rose, try to find a spot where roses have not grown before. The reason for this is a mysterious condition known as Rose Sickness, the result of soil depletion, disease, or other unknown factors that cause a replacement rose to grow less vigorously than the rose that preceded it in the same spot. If you do decide to plant a rose where another rose once grew, remove the soil to a depth and width of two feet and add fresh soil and composted manure.

## Preparing the Soil

Although roses can grow in either alkaline or acidic conditions, they do best in soil with a slightly acid pH of about 5.6 to 6.6. (pH indicates the balance of acidity and alkalinity in soil on a scale of 0 to 14: 0 being completely acidic, 14 being completely alkaline.) If you are not sure of the quality of your soil, test it with a soil-testing kit or send a sample to your state agricultural extension service. If it is too acidic, add lime; if it is too alkaline, add sulfur. Enrich any soil in which roses are to be grown with organic material, such as sphagnum peat moss, to increase organic activity, loosen, and aerate it. This is especially important when the soil is very sandy or heavy with clay. In addition, spread a two-inch layer of rotted cow or horse manure over the entire planting area each year; it can be worked in immediately or allowed to sit through the winter. Be careful with manure that has not aged at least six months: fresh manure can burn the roots and canes if it comes into direct contact with them. Moreover, well-rotted manure is easier to apply.

## How to Plant a Rose

It is best to plant roses on misty, overcast days when there is no danger that sun or wind will dry them out. Soak the entire plant (or bundle of plants if you have bought several bushes) for twenty-four to forty-eight hours in a bucket of muddy water or diluted manure tea (one part rotted manure to eight parts water). Traditionally, muddy water is used because particles of soil, which adhere to the root hairs, help prevent the plant from drying out.

While the roses are soaking, prepare the holes. The growth habit of the varieties you have bought will determine the location and spacing of the plants. As a rule of thumb, large shrubs and climbers should be planted six feet apart. Species roses, which sucker freely, should be given at least this much space. The ideal distance between hybrid teas, floribundas, and grandifloras is one and one-half to two feet, although one foot may suffice. Miniatures may be spaced eight to twelve inches apart. All types of roses grow quickly, and the new growth will fill in the spaces.

Dig each hole approximately twenty-four inches deep and twelve to eighteen inches wide. The hole should be large enough to contain the roots comfortably. For each hole, set aside one spade of rotted or bagged manure and one spade of compost; these will be added later. A medium-sized fish head at the bottom of the hole will provide additional organic nutrients; cover it with about one inch of soil so that it is not in direct contact with the roots.

Remove a rosebush from the water and inspect it. If there are any broken canes or roots, prune them back to the point where the tissue looks healthy. The canes should be green, firm, and smooth, with no shriveled areas; cut off any that are blackened or thinner than a pencil. This is also the time to prune the canes, as they were probably all chopped down to one level in the growing fields just before they were shipped. Cut each one back to a strong, outward-facing bud that has started to swell and looks green and

1. When planting a new rose where another rose once grew, avoid the condition known as Rose Sickness by removing the old soil to a depth and width of two feet.

2. Fill the hole with fresh soil mixed with composted leaves and cow manure.

3. The hole is now ready for the new rose bush.

## Budded Roses

Budding was developed as a way to strengthen tender rose varieties so they are hardy in climates that would not ordinarily be suitable for them. When a bud from a weaker variety, such as a hybrid tea, is grafted to the root system of a more vigorous rose, like a multiflora, the hybrid tea becomes hardier than nature intended because it has the roots of a tougher species rose.

The budding process is quite simple. If a multiflora seedling is to become the rootstock, it is grown outdoors for several years until it is a vigorous plant. Then a bud and a small amount of surrounding stem are cut from a desired rose and inserted under the bark at the base of the stem of the multiflora. The grafted bud fuses with the stem of the more rugged rose and grows into a cane. The multiflora is then pruned back to the bud union, the knob that develops at the point where the bud is attached to the understock. The desired rose now takes over aboveground, while below it the vigorous multiflora roots give it strength.

The Bobbink and Atkins Company of Rutherford, New Jersey, pioneered in the development of successful budded roses in the United States. Lambertus C. Bobbink, a horticulturist from Holland, came to this country in 1895 as a salesman representing a group of Dutch nurserymen. He realized that there was a strong market for roses in America, and he set up his own business here. In 1899 he went into partnership with F. L. Atkins, and they decided that it would be more profitable to sell roses they grew themselves than to import them. Up until that time, American nurserymen, trying to develop roses that would be hardy in all the climates of the United States, had not had much luck with the understock varieties used in England and Europe, such as *R. canina* and the 'Manetti Rose', a Noisette raised in Italy. In 1902, Bobbink and Atkins hit upon the use of *R. multiflora* as an understock, and they were so successful with it that they soon had the first thriving business in field-grown roses in this country.

**1.** Dig a hole that is sufficiently deep and wide to accommodate the roots of the new rose bush.

**2.** Add one spadefull of manure and one spadefull of compost. Mix this well into the hole and the surrounding soil.

**3.** Remove the bare root rose from its package.

**4.** Inspect the new plants for damaged or dead canes and roots. These should be removed. Also prune back tips of strong canes to a healthy bud.

**5.** A grade 1 rose bush should have at least three strong canes and a healthy root stock.

**6.** If you are unable to plant roses when they arrive, you can store them by "heeling them in" to a compost pile. Dig a trench, lay the roses on their sides, and bury them until you are ready to plant them. Roses can be stored over the winter in this manner.

**7.** Before planting a bush, soak it overnight in a bucket of muddy water or a manure tea.

**8.** At planting time, mix the compost and manure well into the bottom of the hole. Create a mound of this soil mix at the bottom of the hole.

**9.** Place the plant in the hole so the roots rest firmly on the soil mix. Make sure there are no air spaces between the roots and the soil. The bud union should be in the proper position for your climate.

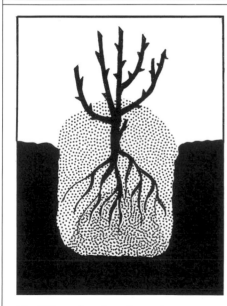

**10.** When the plant is resting firmly on the mound and the bud union is in the proper position, fill the hole with the soil mix. For added protection, build up soil about six inches around the base of the plant.

**11.** Water the plant well, allowing it to settle. Tap the canes lightly to help release any trapped air pockets. Fill in the hole with the remaining soil as the plant settles.

**12.** Build up a ring of soil around the newly planted bush and add more water. This is a good time to start using manure tea or fish emulsion.

Every time you cut roses for your home, you are actually pruning the plant. This encourages new growth that will produce more flowers. Freshly cut roses should be immediately immersed in a bucket of water.

healthy. (Buds, which are sites of new growth, are the swellings that occur at intervals along the canes.) The cut should be at a forty-five-degree angle, with the bud just below the upper edge (see illustration).

Most commercial roses are budded, which means that a desirable rose is grafted to the understock of another, hardier rose. These roses have a distinct bud union, the swollen area at the base of the stem where the rose is joined to the understock (see illustration). The climate in your area will determine how deep the bud union should be planted. If there are long periods of freezing weather, it should be positioned from one to several inches below the level of the soil. This will protect it from the heaving action of the soil caused by alternating freezing and thawing. It will also encourage the plant to produce roots off the desirable canes above the bud union. In warmer regions, such as Texas or Florida, position the bud union above soil level so that any suckers can be easily seen and removed. (Suckers are shoots that develop at the base of the plant. On budded roses, suckers that develop below the bud union originate from the rootstock and can often thrive at the expense of the desirable rose.)

At the bottom of the hole, make a mound

of soil. Put the plant in the hole and spread its roots down over the mound (see illustration). With the bud union at the proper level, hold the plant in place and put enough soil, manure, and compost in the hole to anchor it firmly. Add water, filling to the top of the hole; wait until it soaks through the ground; and then fill the hole to the top with more soil, manure, and compost. In regions where there are extreme climatic changes at planting time, mound up an additional six inches of soil mix around the base of the plant to protect tender buds for a few weeks while the rose adjusts. Finally, make a small trench around the hole and fill it with water rather than soaking the soil close to the plant. Roses planted in the fall should be completely covered with composted leaves and soil, and blanketed with salt hay. In the spring, leave this covering until all danger of frost is past.

Container-grown roses can be planted any time the ground is not frozen. Dig a hole the same size as the container. Combine manure and compost with the soil that was removed. Gently tap the plant out of the container, or cut the container away, being careful not to let the soil fall off the roots; otherwise the plant may go into shock and lose some of its foliage and flowers. Roses bought at local nurseries may be in biodegradable pots that disintegrate in the ground. If so, simply score the sides of the container, cut off the bottom, and plant it without removing the rose.

While waiting for newly planted roses to break leaves and buds, help them along by giving them ample water supplemented with diluted manure tea or fish emulsion. (Fish emulsion: one ounce per gallon; manure tea: one part manure, five parts water.) Keep this mixture handy in a barrel and apply it regularly throughout the season; water and fertilizer promote development and growth of shoots.

## Pruning

The following general rules for pruning apply to all types of roses. Specific techniques and different pruning times for individual classes are discussed in the sections on those roses.

Good pruning tools are a must. For canes of up to about one-half inch in diameter, use

The Cranford Garden, before and after winter pruning.

**1.** All roses, with the exception of some old garden roses, should be pruned at the beginning of the growing season. Rose bushes that are left unpruned will be less productive and prone to disease and insect infestation.

**2.** As a rose bush ages, it becomes crowded with dead wood. This should be removed first. Eliminate the oldest canes, cutting them out at the base of the plant. The newer, healthier, canes have an even color and many swelling buds.

**3.** Roses need good air circulation. Find the center of the plant and open up this area by removing cluttered canes. Cut out any canes that cross each other.

**4.** When pruning modern shrub-type roses such as hybrid teas, floribundas, grandifloras, polyanthas, and shrubs, establish a height that is suitable for your garden. The lower you prune the plant, the stronger the new growth will be.

For the best bloom, hybrid teas should be pruned back by at least two thirds of their height.

**5.** Modern shrub types that are heavily pruned will develop good basal breaks — the strong canes from the base of the plant that produce the best flowers.

**6.** Often, due to winter damage, you will have to prune roses nearly to the ground. Low pruning refers to pruning that results in the removal of two thirds or more of the plant. High pruning means removing less of the plant.

**7.** Make all cuts at a forty-five-degree angle, about one-quarter inch above a swelling or newly breaking bud. The direction in which the bud is pointing is the direction of the new growth. This bud will become a new flower-bearing cane.

**8.** Check carefully the direction of buds, making sure that they are all pointing away from the center of the plant. This important step is known as "shaping" the plant.

**9.** Remove all dead canes. These are easy to see because they are usually blackened and shriveled. Healthy canes are smooth and have an even green or reddish color. Remove any canes that are split or have unusual colors. Unhealthy canes will die as soon as the weather become warm.

**10.** Check carefully for any signs of borers—insects that lay their eggs in exposed tissue of canes. The larvae burrow down the canes, leaving telltale holes. Cut infested canes down to the point where the hole and the borer are completely removed.

**11.** Cut all canes to an even height, as modern shrub-type roses look best when they have uniform growth.

**12.** A healthy plant is one that is correctly pruned to allow for good air circulation and ample room for strong new canes to develop. Pruning time is a good time to add epsom salts to encourage basal break.

**1.** Ramblers, with their pliable canes, are better suited than climbers for training on a low fence. This training should be done immediately after flowering. First remove the older, crowded wood. Then train the new growth in a series of slight curves

over the fence, being careful not to break the canes. **2.** Secure the canes loosely to the fence with soft twine. The further apart the canes are spread and the more horizontal their placement, the more flowers they will produce from tip to base.

sharp secateurs (scissor-action pruning shears with blades that cross) rather than anvil-like pruners, which will crush the canes. For canes that are one to two inches in diameter, use loppers (long-handled pruners). For anything over two inches in diameter, use a small handsaw.

In order to have strong, healthy roses, it is necessary to prune regularly. Basically, this means removing diseased, dead, or unproductive wood, shaping the plant, and making the bush stronger by stimulating new basal growth. The most severe pruning is done at the beginning of the growing season, just before the plants start to grow. In the Cranford Rose Garden this is in late winter or early spring, usually around the middle of March.

First remove dead and diseased wood. Then locate the center of the bush, which is where most of the growth originates. Thin it out so the individual canes have plenty of space: crowding promotes disease and encourages insects. At the same time, shape the bush so that new growth is induced to grow away from the center.

Now start on the remaining canes. Locate a healthy bud that points away from the center of the plant and is swelling and showing signs of growth. At a point about one-quarter inch

above this bud, make a cut at a forty-five-degree angle, with the upper edge of the cut just above the bud (see illustration). This cut will stimulate the remaining buds to grow. A cut too close to the bud will cause its tissue to dry out from exposure to the elements, while a cut too far away will create an area of dead wood that will be vulnerable to insects and disease. If there is time, coat the cut with white glue, wax, or even old lipstick to seal it and keep insects out.

Continue removing faded flowers throughout the season. Bear in mind as you cut spent flowers and flowers for the house that you are also pruning: this is known as deadheading. On repeat-blooming roses this is important for promoting new blooms. If you live in a cold climate, continue pruning up until about a month before the first predicted frost. After that, the tender new growth that results from pruning will die when the weather turns cold.

Many roses need a rest period or they will weaken and die after several years. In northern climates, winter dormancy provides this rest period; but in warmer climates, it must be induced by severe pruning. To determine the proper time for pruning in your area, check with the local rose society.

*Above:* Suckering: Often the rootstock of a budded
rose will begin to send up its own growth from
below the bud union. These suckers are usually
very different from the growth put out by the desirable rose, and they should be cut out immediately.
*Top and right:* The fruits of training efforts.

**1.** Climbing roses develop laterals, branches off the main canes, which bear flowers. At the beginning of the growing season and between periods of bloom, shorten the laterals by two thirds.

**2.** Make the cut as on a regular cane — at a forty-five-degree angle about one-quarter inch above the bud.

**3.** Climbers, unlike ramblers, have very stiff canes. Remove about one third of the oldest wood. This prevents overcrowding and allows room for new growth.

**4.** Climbers tend to become very dense, and they need to be thinned out. They do not send up as many new canes from the base as ramblers.

**5.** Climbers can be trained over fences, on arches, and up walls. To promote the best development of laterals, spread the canes out in a fan shape and space them evenly in a horizontal position.

**6.** Climbers, like ramblers, will not naturally attach themselves to the support, so they should be loosely tied in place.

**1.** It takes time, but climbers and ramblers can be trained to grow up poles. If they are selectively pruned, they will develop beautiful curves.

**2.** Select two or three canes and wrap them around a pole in spiral fashion; this promotes the development of lateral canes. Then wrap them around a chain or rope.

**3.** Before the growing season, while the plant is dormant, or immediately after flowering, carefully wrap the canes around the chain.

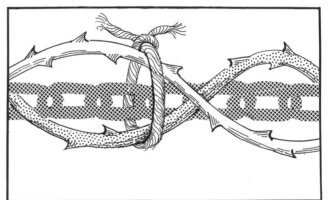

**4.** Wrapping the canes in spiral fashion around the chain promotes development of laterals. Tie them loosely at intervals.

**5.** Climbers, which have stiffer canes than ramblers, need thick supports, such as metal arches. The more pliable canes of ramblers can be trained on chains and slender arches.

**6.** The amount of pruning depends on the growing situation. In formal areas, roses on arches and columns connected by chains should be kept neat and tidy with severe pruning.

**1.** Ramblers grown on arches and pergolas tend to become unruly, and they may block a walkway. They should be pruned immediately after flowering, before diseases and insects have a chance to build up.

**2.** Remove all wood that has just borne flowers, as is being done here with 'Chevy Chase'.

**3.** Carefully remove all old wood from the structure.

**4.** Cut and remove the old wood from the base of the rose. Note that there are plenty of new canes emerging from the base.

**5.** This type of pruning is good for most ramblers, especially 'Dorothy Perkins', 'Excelsa', and 'Chevy Chase'.

**6.** Many climbers that bloom once a season can also be treated in this way, provided they have enough new shoots to replace those that are removed.

**7.** For an archway such as the one shown here, try to leave no more than four to six canes so the rose will not become cluttered.

**8.** Starting with the longest, carefully wrap each cane around the arch. Secure the canes with soft twine, as they will not naturally attach themselves to a support.

**9.** Wrapping makes the rose attractive, and it also helps induce the production of lateral canes that will bear the next season's flowers.

**10.** Whenever possible, wrap both sides of the arch so there will be no bare spots when the canes have filled out with leaves.

**11.** Try to keep the canes from overlapping or rubbing against each other. Tie them all securely with soft twine.

**12.** Now the rambler is neat and has plenty of air circulation. Because they have pliable canes and tidy growth habits, ramblers are easier to train this way than climbers.

LICORICE ROOT

COCOA BEAN HULLS

WOOD CHIPS

WOOD SHAVINGS

▲ SALT MARSH HAY　　　▼ SHREDDED CEDAR BARK

▲ PINE BARK CHIPS　　　▼ PINE NEEDLES

## Fertilizing

Fertilizer stimulates and strengthens new growth. Fertilizers come with differing percentages of nitrogen, phosphorus, and potassium. The choice of fertilizer depends on climate and soil conditions.

In the Cranford Rose Garden, granular fertilizer is applied twice a season: once toward the end of the winter dormant period, and again after the first blooming period. In warmer areas, such as southern Texas and southern California, where roses may not go dormant, fertilizing should be done again after the second flush of flowers. If you are planning to exhibit roses at rose shows, which usually occur at the beginning and end of the rose season, you can improve the quality of your flowers by fertilizing once more about a month before exhibition time.

With a cultivating tool, work a handful of granular fertilizer into the soil around each rosebush. Keep the fertilizer away from the canes and foliage, as it can burn them. Water well after each application.

Foliar feeding, which provides the plant with nutrients that are absorbed rapidly through the leaves, can be done every ten days during the growing season. Liquid seaweed, fish emulsion, or any liquid houseplant fertilizer can be applied to the leaves with a sprayer, either alone or in combination with insecticides and fungicides.

To encourage good basal break (strong canes growing from the bud union at the base of the plant), well-developed flowers later in the season, and good healthy canes that will overwinter well, work two tablespoons of Epsom salts, which contain magnesium for healthy green foliage and strong roots, into the soil around each bush after the first flush of growth and again about one month before frost.

Watch the leaves for symptoms of iron deficiency, characterized by dark veins surrounded by pale green tissue. This condition can be treated with foliar applications of chelated iron, which comes in liquid form.

## Irrigation and Mulching

Roses need plenty of water—at least one inch a

*Opposite:* A variety of mulches

week throughout the growing season. There are many ways to water, from simple hand-held hoses to sophisticated sprinkler and drip systems. Contrary to popular belief, it doesn't hurt to get the leaves of roses wet; just be sure to water early in the day so they will have time to dry out before evening.

Mulches are used to hold moisture in the soil, keep roots cool, and discourage weeds. It is important to remember that the soil under the mulch has to be worked. Mulching without working the soil creates a hard layer of earth that prevents air and water from reaching the roots. In the Cranford Rose Garden, the only mulches used are a dust mulch created by regular soil cultivation and a natural mulch layer formed by two inches of rotted cow manure spread on the beds in winter. If you use mulch, make sure it is material that will break down when it is turned into the soil, such as rotted manure, shredded oak leaves, licorice root, or wood chips. Seed hulls, which are very slow to decompose, are not recommended.

*Above:* The Cranford Garden in winter. *Right:* Tree roses wrapped in burlap.

**1.** In cold climates and at high altitudes, climbing roses should be protected. Take them down from their supports and overwinter them on the ground.

**2.** Remove the climber from its support and, using soft twine, tie the canes together in a bundle.

**3.** Before the ground freezes, dig a trench near the climbing rose's support and lay the canes in the hole, being careful not to disturb the roots.

**4.** Carefully cover the entire plant with soil and mulching material such as oak leaves or salt hay. After the ground freezes, mulch the area heavily. Leave the climbing rose here until early spring.

### *Winter Protection*

In areas where the ground is frozen for any length of time, tender varieties of roses need winter protection. In late autumn, make sure the soil is well watered. When the surface soil begins to freeze, protect weaker, thin-stemmed varieties with a six-inch-high mound of dry soil and coarse, dry, noncompacting organic matter. Shredded oak leaves and salt hay make the best protective material. This mulch will act as insulation to prevent the plants from being damaged by alternating freezing and thawing of the soil. Some people use rose cones, plastic foam caps that cover the entire bush, once the ground is frozen. These need to be well ventilated to prevent diseases from building up inside. Also, before putting on the cones, remove all leaves and diseased canes—diseases can overwinter.

In areas with harsh winters where temperatures are often below zero, release the canes of climbers from their supports, tie them together, bury them in trenches, and cover them with mulch material. In colder climates, standard (tree) roses should be wrapped with mulch or dug up, roots and all, and entirely buried in a trench or compost pile. They may also be potted up and brought into a cool greenhouse or garage for the winter. It is important not to let them dry out.

1. Mulch helps many roses overwinter in areas where the ground freezes during the cold months. Shredded oak leaves make good mulch. Do not use maple or other large leaves.

2. Salt hay and soil can be mixed with the shredded oak leaves.

3. Once the ground is frozen, make a six- to eight-inch mound of mulch around the rose.

4. Cover the mound of mulch with salt hay. Also place salt hay loosely around the canes of more tender roses such as teas and Chinas.

5. Standard, or tree, roses should be wrapped if they are left outdoors during the winter in northern climates. First wrap the entire plant with several inches of salt hay, making sure the salt hay is especi-

ally thick at the point where the bud union is located.
6. Next wrap the rose and the salt hay with burlap to keep the salt hay in place. Leave the plant covered until all danger of frost is past.

## Diseases and Insects

Healthy roses in clean, well-watered, and well-maintained beds will be strong and disease resistant. Diseases can overwinter, so the first line of defense is to keep the beds clean and the bushes spaced far enough apart to allow for good air circulation. Diseases and pests can be kept at an acceptable level in the garden through natural predators and good cultural practices; it is not necessary to completely eradicate them.

There are three categories of disease: fungus (rust, blackspot, powdery mildew, and botrytis), bacteria-related (crown gall), and virus. Rust, blackspot, powdery mildew, and virus are most visible on foliage; botrytis shows up primarily on flowers; and crown gall is usually located at the bases of canes. First remove the diseased parts. Then contact your local American Rose Society chapter, the local agricultural extension service, or the nearest public rose garden to find out which chemical controls work best in your area. If you use fungicides, they must be handled with care. Alternatives to chemicals are now being explored. These involve the use of products such as antidessicants and household disinfectants.

*Rust* occurs when the climate is warm and damp. As its name implies, rust shows up as reddish-brown spots, usually on the undersides of the leaves closest to the ground, and in other areas that tend to remain moist. It can result in yellowing of leaves and defoliation.

*Blackspot*, like rust, thrives when days and nights are warm and humid, especially at times of frequent summer showers. The first signs are small black spots on the leaves. As the disease progresses, yellow rings form around these spots, and eventually the leaves turn completely yellow and fall off. Typically, blackspot starts at the bottom of a plant and works its way up. It can defoliate and weaken an entire rosebush.

*Powdery mildew* is prevalent in areas where days are warm and nights cool, especially when there is poor air circulation and high humidity. The first sign is curling and distortion of the youngest leaves. Later, a layer of grayish fungus coats the leaves, leaf stalks, flowers, stems, and buds—particularly on new growth at the top of the bush. Powdery mildew will not usually cause defoliation, but it can kill the tips of young canes, hinder flower development, and cause flower buds to fall off. Washing plants early in the morning helps control this fungus.

*Botrytis blight* affects the petals of roses that have large, many-petaled flowers, such as centifolias. This fungus spreads when cool weather suddenly turns warm and humid. It gets into the closed petals and prevents the buds from opening (this is called balling). The flowers begin to rot from the inside, and the outer petals become brown and moldy. Prompt deadheading helps prevent the spread of this disease.

*Crown gall* is the most common bacterial problem on roses. It is a growth on the bud union that is not easy to see when the union is planted below soil level. Resembling the head of a cauliflower, it eventually envelops the bud union as well as the area around the canes at the base of the plant and kills the rosebush. If you catch crown gall in the early stages, you can cut it out with a knife and treat the infected area with a mild solution of chlorine bleach.

Knives and all tools that come into contact with crown gall or other diseases should be cleaned with rubbing alcohol so the problems are not spread to other plants.

*Rose mosaic*, which has recently been recognized as a major problem in the rose industry, is a disease caused by a virus. The symptoms are yellow and green lines or patterns on foliage. Apparently it originates during the budding process in nurseries, and it can be prevented only at the nurseries, for it is not spread in the garden by pruning or insects. It eventually affects flower production and causes general decline in the health of the plant.

## Insects

Insects will be deterred if healthy roses are grown in clean beds. If insects do attack, first try to get rid of them with organic materials, such as nondetergent soaps. For advice on the use of chemicals, contact your local American Rose Society chapter, the local agricultural extension service, or the nearest public rose garden. Organic and chemical controls are available at your local nursery.

*Aphids* are the first insects of the season to attack roses, at least in the Northeast. They are small, sucking insects that like cool weather and tender new growth, especially around flower buds. They can cause deformities and stunted blooms. Insecticides will kill them, but first try to knock them off with strong jets of water.

*Japanese beetles* are shiny copper-green beetles that eat through closed rose buds, searching for nectar and pollen and leaving holes in all the petals. They can consume the entire flower as well as the foliage. They attack all types of roses, but they are more noticeable on those with light-colored flowers. In early spring and late summer, you can kill the grubs (the larvae of Japanese beetles) by treating soil and lawn areas with grub-killing insecticides. You can also spray the plants with insecticides, but the beetles will not die unless they are directly hit by the poison. One of the best ways to control Japanese beetles is to pick them off the plants by hand and drop them into water. There is also an effective biological control, milky spore, a bacterium that needs time to build up in the soil.

*Midges,* which are most prevalent during the summer bloom period, are the tiny larvae of small flies. These flies lay their eggs in the young growing leaves, flower buds, and flower stalks. As the larvae grow and feed on this tissue, they cause the leaves and buds to be deformed, severely bent, and often blackened. Later, the larvae fall off into the flower beds, where they mature and repeat the cycle. At the first sign of this problem, prune off all affected parts and burn or dispose of the debris, making sure it does not go into the compost pile, where it could spread. Keep flower beds scrupulously clean, and treat plants and beds with an insecticide recommended for midge control. The fly has a short life cycle, so the application should be repeated in five days.

*Thrips,* tiny orange insects that are usually a problem in warmer climates and in greenhouses, cause buds to remain closed or flowers to be disfigured with brownish streaks, spots, and bumps. Thrips seem to prefer light-colored roses; at least they are more noticeable on them. Systemic insecticide, applied either by foliar application or through the soil, is the best treatment.

*Spider mites* generally occur when the weather turns hot and dry. The affected leaves look dull, desiccated, yellow-orange, and dusty, and they have webbing and little specks, which are the mites, on the undersides. The first thing to do is spray the entire bush from the bottom up with cold water; if done regularly, this may control the mites, which can't tolerate water, before they get out of hand. Once the webbing has built up, however, the problem is serious and a miticide is necessary.

*Borers* are the larvae of various flying insects that enter rose canes through wounds or pruning cuts. They bore or tunnel their way down the canes, causing them to brown, wilt, and die back. Affected canes will be hollow; cut them back to healthy tissue. To prevent borers from reentering the canes, seal the tips with white glue or wax.

Gardens

CHAPTER

*6*

*Rose Gardens*

*Since the establishment in 1904 of the first municipal
rose garden in the United States (Elizabeth Park, Hartford,
Connecticut), hundreds of rose gardens in all parts of the
country have opened to the public. Some of the gardens listed
here have thousands of plants; others have small but impressive
collections of select varieties, such as species or old
garden roses. A public rose garden is one of the best places
to find out which roses grow well in your area. There you
can also see the wide range of varieties that are available
and learn how to use them in different types of
gardens and landscapes.*

*Preceding pages:* The Rudolf W. Van der Goot Rose Garden, East Millstone, NJ

## ALABAMA

**Birmingham Botanical Gardens**
2616 Lane Park Road
Birmingham 25223
205-879-1227
*1,200 plants, 153 varieties*

**Fairhope City Rose Garden**
1 Fairhope Avenue
Fairhope 36533
205-928-8003
1,200 plants, 35 varieties
*AARS Display Garden*

**David A. Hemphill Park of Roses**
**Mobile Public Rose Garden**
Springdale Plaza, Airport Blvd.
Mobile 36606
205-479-3775
*800 + plants, 300 varieties*
*AARS Garden*

**Bellingrath Rose Garden**
Rte 1, Box 60
Theodore 36582
205-973-2217
*2,800 plants, 35 varieties*
*AARS Garden*

## ARIZONA

**Sahuaro Historical Ranch Rose Garden**
9802 N. 59th Avenue
Glendale 85302
602-931-5622
*1,500 plants, 100 varieties*
*AARS Garden*

**Valley Garden Center**
1809 N. 15th Avenue
Phoenix 85007
602-461-7055
*1,255 plants, 100 varieties*
*AARS Garden*

**Gene C. Reid Park**
900 S. Randolph Way
Tucson 85716
(602) 791-4873
*1,080 plants, 138 varieties*
*AARS Garden*

## ARKANSAS

**State Capitol Rose Garden**
State Capitol Building
Little Rock 72201
501-371-5176
*1,400 plants, 75 varieties*
*AARS Garden*

## CALIFORNIA

**Los Angeles State and County**
**Arboretum**
301 North Baldwin Avenue
Arcadia 91007
818-446-8251
*80 + plants*
*Old-fashioned roses*

**Virginia Robinson Gardens**
Beverly Hills
(Exact location disclosed when reservations are made.)
213-276-5367
*200 plants, 70 varieties*

**Fountain Square Rose Garden**
7115 Greenback Lane
Citrus Heights 95621
916-969-6666
*402 plants, 157 varieties*
*AARS Garden*

**Roger's Gardens**
2301 San Joaquin Hills Road
Corona del Mar 92625
714-640-5800
*36 plants, 36 varieties*
*AARS Garden*

**Sherman Library and Gardens**
2647 East Coast Highway
Corona del Mar 92625
714-673-2261
*36 plants, 18 varieties*

**Bella Rosa Winery Rose Garden**
Pond Road and Highway 99
DeLano 93215
805-831-5197
*1,263 plants, 88 varieties*
*AARS Garden*

**Quail Botanical Gardens**
230 Quail Gardens Drive
Encinitas, CA 92024
619-436-8301
*10 plants, 9 varieties*
*Specializes in tender varieties, Chinas, and Noisettes.*

**Descanso Gardens Rose Garden**
1418 Descanso Drive
La Canada 91011
818-790-5571
*4,000 plants, 150 varieties*
*Species dating back to 1200 B.C. in the Old Fashioned Rose Garden; varieties in succeeding historical periods are planted in labeled groups.*
*AARS Garden*

Bellingrath Rose Garden, Theodore, Alabama

**Exposition Park Rose Garden**
701 State Drive
Los Angeles  90037
213-748-4772
*15,000 plants, 145 varieties*
*AARS Garden*

**J. Paul Getty Museum**
17985 Pacific Coast Highway
Malibu 90625
213-459-7611
*110 plants, 3 varieties*
*Museum and gardens are a recreation of the*
*Villa dei Papiri at Herculaneum which was*
*destroyed by the eruption of Mt. Vesuvius in*
*A.D. 79.*

**Morcom Amphitheater of Roses**
700 Jean Street
Oakland 94610
415-658-0731
*5,000 plants, 300 varieties*
*AARS Garden*

**South Coast Botanic Garden**
26300 Crenshaw Boulevard
Palos Verdes Peninsula 90274
213-544-1948
*400 plants*
*This is the first garden ever built on a sanitary*
*landfill*

**Tournament of Roses Wrigley Garden**
391 S. Orange Grove Blvd.
Pasadena 91184
818-449-4100
*1,500 plants, 100 varieties*
*AARS Garden*

**Rose Bowl Rose Garden**
1001 Rose Bowl Drive
Pasadena 91103
818-577-3100
*2,500 plants*
*AARS Garden*

**Fairmount Park Rose Garden**
2225 Market Street
Riverside 92501
714-782-5401
*1,350 plants, 78 varieties*
*AARS Garden*

**McKinley Park Rose Garden**
601 Alhambra Blvd.
Sacramento 95816
916-448-4273
*1,200 plants, 158 plants*
*AARS Garden*

**Capitol Park Rose Garden**
1300 L Street
Sacramento 85814
916-445-3658
*1,500 plants, 60 varieties*
*AARS Garden*

**Inez Curant Parker Rose Garden**
2130 Pan American Plaza
San Diego 92101
619-236-5717
*2,000 plants, 200 varieties*
*AARS Garden*

**Golden Gate Park Rose Garden**
Golden Gate Park
San Francisco 94117
415-666-7003
*1,500 plants, 145 varieties*
*AARS Garden*

**San Jose Municipal Rose Garden**
Nagles and Dana Avenues
San Jose 95121
408-287-0698
*4,500 plants, 158 varieties*
*AARS Garden*

**Huntington Botanical Gardens**
1151 Oxford Road
San Marino 91108
818-405-2100
*4,000 plants, 1,800 varieties*
*Garden is centered on a "rose history walk"*
*AARS Garden*

**Hearst San Simeon State Historical
Monument**
750 Hearst Castle Road
San Simeon 93452
805-927-2090
*2300 plants, 80 varieties*

**A.C. Postel Memorial Rose Garden**
Los Olives and Laguna Streets
Santa Barbara 93103
805-564-5437
*1,300 plants, 130 varieties*
*AARS Garden*

**Westminster Civic Center Rose Garden**
8200 Westminster Blvd.
Westminster 92683
714-895-2860
*1,440 plants, 162 varieties*
*AARS Garden*

**Wasco Community Garden**
Barker Park
11th Street at Birch
Wasco 93280
*1,000 plants*

**Pageant of Roses Garden**
3900 S. Workman Mill Road
Whittier 90601
213-692-1212
*6,000 plants, 600 varieties*
*AARS Garden*

**Filoli Center**
Canada Road
Woodside 94062
415-364-8300
*560 plants, 250 varieties*
*by reservation only*

COLORADO

**Four Corners Rose Garden**
E. 2nd Avenue and 12th Street
Durango 81301
*300 plants*

**War Memorial Rose Garden**
5804 S. Bemis Street
Littleton 80120
303-795-9856
*800 plants, 7 varieties*
*AARS Garden*

**Longmont Memorial Rose Garden**
Roosevelt Park
700 Longs Peak
Longmont 80501
303-651-8446
*1,130 plants, 68 varieties*
*AARS Garden*

CONNECTICUT

**Norwich Memorial Rose Garden**
Mohegan Park
Rockwell Street and Judd Road
Norwich 06360
203-886-2381
*2,500 plants, 200 varieties*
*AARS Garden*

**Elizabeth Park Rose Garden**
150 Walbridge Road
Hartford 06119
203-722-6543
*1,500 plants, 800 varieties*
*The first municipal rose garden in America.*
*AARS Garden*

Huntington Botanical Gardens, San Marino, California

## DELAWARE

**Hagley Museum and Library**
PO Box 3630
Wilmington 19807
305-658-2400
*95 plants, 20 varieties*
*The E.I. du Pont Restored Garden contains a small rose garden with nineteenth century roses.*

## DISTRICT OF COLUMBIA

**The George Washington University**
2033 G Street NW and 730 21st Street
Washington 20052
202-994-7575
*600 plants, 90 varieties*
*AARS Garden*

**United States Botanic Garden**
Maryland Avenue and First Street SW
Washington 20052
202-225-7099
*180 plants, 30 varieties*

**Dumbarton Oaks**
1703 32nd Street NW
Washington 20052
202-342-3200
*1000 plants, 35 varieties*

## FLORIDA

**Walt Disney World Company Rose Garden**
PO Box 10,000
Lake Buena Vista 32830
407-824-6256
*900 plants, 39 varieties*
*AARS Garden*

**Sturgeon Memorial Rose Garden**
13401 Indian Rocks Road
Largo 34644
*850 plants, 125 varieties*
*AARS Garden*

**Florida Cypress Gardens**
PO Box 1
Cypress Gardens 33884
813-324-2111
*200 plants, 12 varieties*
*AARS Garden*

**Giles Rose Nursery**
2966 State Road 710
Okeechobee, 33472
*813-763-7579*
*3,000 plants*

## GEORGIA

**Elizabeth Bradley Turner Memorial Rose Garden**
State Botanical Gardens of Georgia
2450 S. Milledge Road
Athens 30605
404-542-1244
*480 plants, 123 varieties*
*AARS Garden*

**Atlanta Botanical Garden**
PO Box 77246, Piedmont Park at the Prado
Atlanta 30357
404-876-5859
*600 plants, 44 varieties*
*AARS Garden*

**Rose Test Garden**
1840 Smith Avenue
Thomasville 31792
912-226-5568
*2,000 plants, 250 varieties*
*One section of garden is devoted to testing new varieties, balance is planted with varieties especially well-suited to the South.*
*AARS Garden*

## HAWAII

**University of Hawaii**
Maui County Research
End of Mauna Place
Kula, Maui 96790
808-878-1213
*432 plants, 22 varieties*
*AARS Garden*

## IDAHO

**Julia Davis Memorial Rose Garden**
The River and Capital Boulevard
Boise
208-344-5515
*900 plants*

## ILLINOIS

**The Nan Elliot Memorial Rose Garden**
The Gordon F. Moore Community Park
4550 College Avenue
Alton 62002
618-463-3580
*1,700 plants, 130 varieties*
*AARS Garden*

**Marquette Park**
6700 South Kedzie Avenue
Chicago 60629
312-776-0728
*4,500 plants, 75 varieties*

**Merrick Park Rose Garden**
S.W. Corner of Oak Avenue and Lake
Street
Evanston 60204
312-866-2911
*2,000 plants, 90 varieites*
*AARS Garden*

**The Bruce Krasberg Rose Garden**
Chicago Botanic Garden
Lake Cook Road, P O Box 400
Glencoe 60022
312-835-5441
*5,000 plants, 162 varieties*
*Roses that perform well in Chicago area*
*AARS Garden*

**Park District of Highland Park**
636 Ridge Road
Highland Park 60035
312-831-3810
*380 plants, 32 varieties*

**Lynn J. Arthur Rose Garden**
Cook Memorial Park
Libertyville 60064
312-937-7896
*772 plants, 68 varieties*
*AARS Garden*

**Morton Arboretum**
Route 53
Lisle 60532
708-968-0074
*378 plants, 83 varieties*
*Low-maintenance, winter-hardy rose varieties.*
*Various methods of winter protection tested.*
*Minimal use of sprays.*

**George L. Luthy Memorial Botanical**
**Garden**
2218 North Prospect Road
Peoria 61603
309-686-3362
*1,000 plants, 128 varieties*
*AARS Garden*

**Rockford Park District**
Sinnissippi Greenhouse and Gardens
1401 North Second Street
Rockford 61107
815-987-8858
*3,500 plants, 74 varieties*
*Center of rose garden has a 32-foot floral clock*
*AARS Garden*

**Washington Park Rose Garden**
Fayette and Chatham Road
P O Box 5052
Springfield 62705
217-787-2540
*3,000 plants, 230 varieties*
*AARS Garden*

**Cantigny Gardens**
1 South 151 Winfield Road
Wheaton 60187
708-668-5161
*1,000 plants, 100 varieties*
*AARS Garden*

INDIANA

**Lakeside Rose Garden**
Lakeside Park
1500 Lake Avenue
Fort Wayne 46805
219-427-1253
*2,000 plants, 225 varieties*
*Features a large pergola with old ramblers,*
*reflecting pools, a floral sundial.*
*AARS Garden*

**Richmond Rose Garden**
Glen Miller Park
Richmond 47374
*1,600 plants, 90 varieties*
*AARS Garden*

IOWA

**Iowa State University Horticultural**
**Garden**
Pammel Drive and Haber Road
Ames 50011
515-294-0038
*670 plants, 134 varieties*
*AARS Garden*

**Bettendorf Park Board Municipal Rose**
**Garden**
2204 Grant Street
Bettendorf 52722
319-359-0913
*617 plants, 42 varieties*
*AARS Garden*

**Noelridge Park Rose Garden**
4900 Council Street N.E.
Cedar Rapids 52402
319-398-5101
*540 plants, 43 plants*
*AARS Garden*

**Bickelhaupt Arboretum**
340 South 14th Street
Clinton 52732
319-242-4771
*37 plants, 30 varieties*

**Vander Veer Park Municipal Rose**
**Garden**
215 West Central Park Avenue
Davenport 52803
319-326-7865
*2,300 plants, 170 varieties*
*AARS Garden*

**Greenwood Park Rose Garden**
Greenwood Park
Des Moines 50316
515-271-4708
*2,500 plants, 280 varieties*
*AARS Garden*

**Dubuque Aboretum and Botanical**
**Gardens**
3125 W. 32nd Street and Aboretum Drive
Dubuque 52001
319-582-8621
*725 plants, 200 varieties*
*AARS Garden*

**Weed Park Memorial Rose Garden**
Weed Park
Muscatine 52761
319-263-0241
*1,300 plants, 85 varieties*
*AARS Garden*

**State Center Public Rose Garden**
300 3rd Street SE
State Center 50247
515-483-2081
*1,500 plants, 100 varieties*
*AARS Garden*

Walt Disneyworld Rose Garden, Orlando, Florida

**E.F.A. Reinisch Rose Garden**
Gage Park
4320 West 10th Street
Topeka 66604
913-272-6150
*6,500 plants, 400 variations*
*AARS Garden*

**Lake Shawnee Gardens**
West Edge Drive at E. 37th Street
Topeka 66609
913-267-2000
*680 plants*

KENTUCKY

**Kentucky Memorial Rose Garden**
Kentucky Fair and Exposition Center
Louisville 40232
502-267-6308
*1,300 plants, 91 varieties*
*AARS Garden*

LOUISIANA

**Louisiana State University Rose Variety**
**Test Garden**
4560 Essen Lane
Baton Rouge 70809
504-766-3471
*2,000 plants, 344 varieties*
*AARS Garden*

**Hodges Gardens**
PO Box 900
Highway 171 South
Many 71449
318-586-4806
*3,600 plants, 125 varieties*
*AARS Garden*

**American Rose Center**
8877 Jefferson-Paige Road
Shreveport 71119
318-938-5402
*300 plants, 15 varieties*
*AARS Garden*

MAINE

**City of Portland Rose Circle**
Derring Oaks Park
Portland 04101
207-775-5451
*700 plants, 31 varieties*
*AARS Garden*

*Opposite:* Ladew Topiary Gardens, Monkton, Maryland

## MARYLAND

**William Paca Garden**
1 Martin Street
Annapolis 21401
301-267-6656
*100 plants, 13 varieties*
*This 2-acre restored 18th-century garden*
*features a parterre designed to display a*
*collection of old roses.*

**Maryland Rose Society Heritage Rose
Garden**
The Clyburn Arboretum
4915 Greenspring Avenue
Baltimore 21209
301-396-0180
*29 plants, 12 varieties*

**Ladew Topiary Gardens**
3535 Jarrettsville Pike
Monkton 21111
301-557-9570
*250 plants, 30 varieties*

**Brookside Botanical Gardens Rose
Garden**
1500 Glenallen Avenue
Wheaton 20902
301-949-8231
*700 plants, 64 varieties*
*AARS Garden*

## MASSACHUSETTS
**James P. Kelleher Rose Garden**
Park Drive
Boston 02130
617-524-3362
*2,000 plants, 103 varieties*
*AARS Garden*

**Arnold Arboretum of Harvard
University**
125 Arborway
Jamaica Plain 02130
617-524-1721
*1,302 plants, 165 varieties*
*Roses are planted in thickets and colonies — not*
*in rows — as they might occur in nature*

**Berkshire Garden Center**
PO Box 826, Route 102
Stockbridge 01262
413-298-3926
*Rose garden under renovation*

**Naumkeag**
P.O. Box 792, Prospect Hill
Stockbridge 01262
413-298-3239
*128 plants, 16 varieties*

**The Stanley Park of Westfield, Inc.**
400 Western Avenue
Westfield 01085
413-568-9312
*2,000 plants, 50 varieties*
*AARS Garden*

## MICHIGAN

**Matthaei Botanical Gardens**
1800 Dixboro Road
Ann Arbor 48105
313-763-7060
*165 plants, 55 varieties*

**Anna Scripps Whitcomb Conservatory**
Belle Isle
Detroit 48207
313-267-7133
*85 plants, 10 varieties*
*Started June, 1988.*

**Michigan State University
Demonstration Gardens**
Horticulture Department
East Lansing 48823
517-355-0348
*500 plants, 120 varieties*
*AARS Garden*

**Frances Park Memorial Rose Garden**
2600 Moores River Drive
Lansing 48912
517-483-4207
*1,100 plants, 150 roses*
*AARS Garden*

**Fernwood Botanic Gardens**
13988 Rangeline Road
Niles 49120
*50 plants, 25 varieties*
*Roses are incorporated into naturalized*
*landscape features and erosion control.*

## MINNESOTA

**Minnesota Landscape Arboretum**
3675 Arboretum Drive, PO Box 39
Chanhassen 55317
*500 plants, 350 varieties*
*The Arboretum is currently working on the*
*development of hardy roses for northern climates,*
*specifically varieties with continual bloom or*
*rebloom and varieties that do not need winter*
*protection.*

**Lyndale Park Municipal Rose Garden**
4125 East Lake Harriet Parkway
Minneapolis 55409
612-348-4448
*3,000 plants, 150 varieties*
*AARS Garden*

**Como Park Conservatory**
Midway Parkway and Kaufman Drive
St. Paul 55103
612-489-5378
*75 potted plants, 10 varieties*

## MISSISSIPPI

**Hattiesburg Area Rose Society Garden**
University of S. Mississippi
Hattiesburg 39401
601-583-8848
*1,200 plants, 40 varieties*
*AARS Garden*

## MISSOURI

**Cape Girardeau Rose Display Garden**
Park Street
Cape Girardeau 63701
314-335-0706
*700 plants, 40 varieties*
*AARS Garden*

**Laura Conyers Smith Municipal Rose Garden**
Jacob L. Loose Memorial Park
52nd & Pennsylvania
Kansas City 63110
816-333-6706
*3,500 plants, 90 varieties*
*AARS Garden*

**Gladney & Lehmann Rose Gardens**
Missouri Botanical Garden
4344 Shaw Boulevard
St. Louis 63110
314-577-5100
*5,000 plants, 200 varieties*
*AARS Garden*

## MONTANA

**Missoula Memorial Rose Garden**
Blaine & Brooks Street
Missoula 59833
406-642-3340
*326 plants, 52 varieties*
*AARS Garden*

## NEBRASKA

**AARS Constitution Rose Garden**
Father Flanagan's Boys' Home
Boys Town 68010
402-498-1104
*800 Plants, 44 varieties*
*AARS Garden*

**Lincoln Municipal Rose Garden**
Antelope Park
27th and C Street
Lincoln 68502
402-471-7847
*700 plants, 37 varieties*
*AARS Garden*

**Hanscom Park Greenhouse**
1500 South 32nd Street
Omaha 68105
402-444-5497
*1,582 plants, 175 varieties*

**Memorial Park Rose Garden**
57th and Underwood Avenue
Omaha 68104
402-444-5497
*1,600 plants; 162 varieties*
*AARS Garden*

## NEVADA

**Reno Municipal Rose Garden**
2055 Idlewild Drive
Reno 89509
702-785-2270
*2,400 plants, 560 varieties*
*AARS Garden*

## NEW HAMPSHIRE

**Fuller Gardens Rose Gardens**
10 Willow Avenue
North Hampton 03862
603-964-5414
*1,400 plants, 100 varieties*
*AARS Garden*

## NEW JERSEY

**Rudolf W. van der Goot Rose Garden**
Colonial Park
R.D. 1, Mettler's Road
East Millstone 08873
201-873-2549
*4,000 plants, 275 varieties*
*AARS Garden*

**Lambertus C. Bobbink Memorial Rose Garden**
Thompson Park
Newman Springs Road
Lincoln 07738
201-842-4000
*770 plants, 63 varieties*
*AARS Garden*

**Freylinghuysen Arboretum**
53 E. Hanover Ave, PO Box 1295
Morristown 07962
201-326-7600
*150 plants, 27 varieties*
*Small collection of heritage roses.*

Frances Park Memorial Rose Garden, Lansing, Michigan

**Reeves-Reed Arboretum**
165 Hobart Avenue
Summit 07901
201-273-8787
*204 plants, 57 varieties*

**Jack D. Lissemore Rose Garden**
Davis Johnson Park & Gardens
137 Engle Street
Tenafly 07670
*1,235 plants, 75 varieties*
*AARS Garden*

NEW MEXICO

**Prospect Park Rose Garden**
8205 Apache Avenue NE
Alburquerque 87110
505-296-8210
*1,200 plants, 500 varieties*
*AARS Garden*

NEW YORK

**The Peggy Rockefeller Rose Garden**
The New York Botanical Garden
Bronx 10458
212-220-8767
*2,700 plants, 238 varieties*
*Roses are planted by type for comparability*
*AARS Garden*

**The Cranford Rose Garden**
Brooklyn Botanic Garden
1000 Washington Avenue
Brooklyn 11225
718-622-4433
*6,000 plants, 1,100 varieties*
*AARS Garden*

Rudolf W. van der Goot Rose Garden, East Millstone, New Jersey

**Joan Fuzak Memorial Rose Garden**
502 City Hall
Buffalo 14202
716-815-4268
*1,000 plants, 250 varieties*
*AARS Garden*

**Sonnenberg Gardens Rose Garden**
151 Charlotte Street
Canadaigua 14424
716-394-2521
*2,600 plants, 35 varieties*
*AARS Garden*

**Queens Botanical Garden**
43-50 Main Street
Flushing New York
718-886-3800
*230 plants, 42 varieties*
*AARS Garden*

**The Cloisters**
The Metropolitan Museum of Art
Fort Tryon Park 10040
212-923-3700
*8 plants, 8 varieties*
*Medieval roses, grown and known in Europe*
*during the middle ages.*

**United Nations Rose Garden**
United Nations
New York   10017
212-963-6145
*1,391 plants, 39 varieties*
*AARS Garden*

**Old Westbury Gardens**
Old Westbury Road
P.O. Box 430
Old Westbury, 11568
516-333-0048
*440 plants, 24 varieties*
*AARS Garden*

**Maplewood Rose Garden**
100 Maplewood Avenue
Rochester 14163
716-244-8079
*3,000 plants, 210 varieties*
*AARS Garden*

**Central Park Rose Garden**
Central Parkway
Schnectady 12305
518-382-5152
*4,000 plants, 80 varieties*
*AARS Garden*

Peggy Rockefeller Rose Garden, The New York Botanical Garden, Bronx, New York

**E.M. Mills Memorial Rose Garden**
Thornden Park
Ostron Avenue and University Place
Syracuse 13207
315-473-2631
*2,500 plants, 112 varieties*
*AARS Garden*

## NORTH CAROLINA

**Biltmore Estate**
1 North Park Square
Asheville 28801
704-255-1776
*2,000 plants, 80 varieties*
*AARS Garden*

**Tanglewood Park Rose Garden**
Tanglewood Park
P.O. Box 1040
Clemmons 27012
919-766-0591
*857 plants, 72 varieties*
*AARS Garden*

**Fayetteville Rose Garden**
Fayetteville Technical Community College
2201 Hull Road
Fayetteville 28303
919-323-1961
*960 plants, 38 varieties*
*AARS Garden*

**Raleigh Municipal Rose Garden**
301 Pogue Street
Raleigh 27607
919-821-4579
*1,200 plants, 60 varieties*
*AARS Garden*

**Reynolda Rose Gardens of Wake Forest University**
100 Reynolda Village
Winston-Salem 27106
919-759-5593
*1,050 plants, 90 varieties*
*AARS Garden*

## NORTH DAKOTA

**International Peace Garden, Inc.**
Rte 1, PO Box 116
Dunseith 58329
701-263-4390
*50 plants, 16 varieties*
*Concentrates on hardy northern varieties*

## OHIO

**Stan Hywet Hall and Gardens**
714 North Portage Path
Akron 44303
216-836-0576
*800 plants, 60 varieties*
*AARS Garden*

**Cahoon Memorial Rose Garden**
Cahoon Memorial Park
Bay Village 44140
216-871-5081
*1,250 plants, 190 varieties*
*AARS Garden*

**Mary Anne Sears Sweetland Rose Garden**
Garden Center of Greater Cleveland
11030 East Boulevard
Cleveland 44106
*208 plants, 30 varieties*

**Columbus Park of Roses**
3923 North High Street
Columbus 43214
614-645-3350
*9,773 plants, 322 varieties*
*Annual Rose Festival*
*AARS Garden*

**Charles E. Nail Memorial Rose Garden**
Kingwood Center
900 Park Avenue West
Mansfield 44906
419-522-0211
*850 plants, 250 varieties*
*AARS Garden*

**Inniswood Metro Gardens**
940 Hempstead Road
Westerville 43081
614-895-6216
*417 plants, 140 varieties*

**Secrest Arboretum**
Ohio State University
1680 Madison Avenue
Wooster 44691
216-263-3761
*1,297 plants, 445 varieties*

## OKLAHOMA

**J.E. Conrad Municipal Rose Garden**
641 Park Drive
Muskogee 74401
918-682-6602
*2,500 plants, 236 varieties*
*AARS Garden*

**Charles E. Sparks Rose Garden**
3500 Pat Murphy Drive
Will Rogers Park
Oklahoma City 73112
405-943-4200
*4,000 plants, 300 varieties*
*AARS Garden*

**Tulsa Municipal Rose Garden**
Woodward Park
21st and Peoria
Tulsa 74114
918-747-2709
*9,000 plants, 291 varieties*
*AARS Garden*

---

OREGON

**Shore Acres Botanical Gardens/State Park**
13030 Cape Arago Highway
Coos Bay 97420
503-888-3732
*726 plants, 65 varieties*
*AARS Garden*

**Corvallis Rose Garden**
Avery Park
Corvallis 97330
503-753-8164
*1,400 plants, 300 varieties*
*AARS Garden*

**Owen Memorial Rose Garden**
300 North Jefferson
Eugene 97401
503-687-5334
*4,500 plants, 450 varieties*
*AARS Garden*

**International Rose Test Garden**
400 S.W. Kingston Avenue
Portland 97201
503-248-4302
*10,000 plants, 450 varieties*
*AARS Garden*

---

PENNSYLVANIA

**Malcolm W. Gross Memorial Rose Garden**
2700 Parkway Boulevard
Allentown 18104
215-437-7628
*3,600 plants, 80 varieties*
*AARS Garden*

**Hershey Gardens**
P.O. Box B6, Hotel Road
Hershey 17033
717-534-3492
*8,000 plants, 300 varieties*
*AARS Garden*

**Longwood Gardens, Inc.**
Dept. of Horticulture,
Rte 1, P.O. Box 501
Kennett Square 19348
215-388-6741
*1,200 plants, 100 varieties*
*Indoor roses displayed autumn through spring*
*AARS Garden*

**Marion Rivanus Rose Garden**
Morris Arboretum
University of Pennsylvania
9414 Meadowbrook Avenue
Philadelphia 19118
215-247-5777
*1,000 plants, 50 varieties*

**Robert Pyle Memorial Gardens**
Rtes 1 and 796
West Grove 19390
215-869-2426
*2,100 plants, 100 varieties*

---

RHODE ISLAND

**Blithewold Gardens and Arboretum**
Ferry Road
Bristol 02809
401-253-2707
*70 plants, 10 varieties*
*Excellent specimen of* Rosa Roxburghii

**Rosecliff**
Bellevue Avenue
Newport 02840
401-846-7718
*200 plants, 4 varieties*

---

SOUTH CAROLINA

**Edisto Memorial Gardens**
200 Riverside Drive
Orangeburg 29115
803-534-6376
*3,100 plants, 75 varieties*
*AARS Garden*

---

SOUTH DAKOTA

**Rapid City Memorial Rose Garden**
444 Mt. Rushmore Road
Rapid City 57702
605-394-4175
*875 plants, 71 varieties*
*AARS Garden*

Columbus Park of Roses, Columbus, Ohio

**Warner Park Rose Garden**
1254 East Third Street
Chattanooga 37404
615-757-5054
*1,100 plants, 100 varieties*
*AARS Garden*

**Memphis Municipal Rose Garden**
750 Cherry Road
Audobon Park
Memphis 38117
901-685-1566
*1,500 plants, 70 varieties*
*AARS Garden*

**Cheekwood Botanical Gardens**
Forrest Park Drive
Nashville 37205
615-353-2148
*500 plants, 49 varieties*

TEXAS

**Mabel Davis Rose Garden**
Zilker Botanical Gardens
2220 Barton Springs Road
Austin 78749
512-478-6875
*850 plants, 62 varieties*
*AARS Garden*

**Dallas Arboretum and Botanical Gardens**
8617 Garland Road
Dallas 75218
214-327-8263
*100 plants*

**Samuell-Grand Municipal Rose Garden**
6200 East Grand Boulevard
Dallas 75218
214-826-4540
*4,750 plants, 270 varieties*
*AARS Garden*

**El Paso Municipal Rose Garden**
1702 North Copia
(Corner of Copia and Aurora Streets)
El Paso 79904
505-755-2555
*1,414 plants, 223 varieties*
*AARS Garden*

**Fort Worth Botanic Gardens**
3220 Botanic Garden Drive
Fort Worth 76107
817-870-7688
*3,820 plants, 190 varieties*
*AARS Garden*

**Houston Municipal Rose Garden**
1500 Hermann Drive
Houston 77004
713-529-3960
*2,400 plants, 97 varieties*
*AARS Garden*

**Tyler Municipal Rose Garden**
420 South Rose Park
Tyler 75702
214-531-1200
*30,000 plants, 400 varieties*
*AARS Garden*

**Victoria Rose Garden**
480 McCright Drive
Victoria 77901
512-572-2767
*1,000 plants, 110 varieties*

---

UTAH

**USU/Utah Botanical Garden**
817 North Main
Farmington 84025
801-451-3204
*490 plants, 228 varieties*

**Territorial Statehouse State Park Rose Garden**
50 West Capitol Avenue
Fillmore 84631
801-743-5316
*250 plants, 75 varieties*
*AARS Garden*

**The Nephi Federated Women's Club Memorial Rose Garden**
1 North 1 East
Nephi 84648
801-623-2003
*1,000 plants, 100 varieties*
*AARS Garden*

Biltmore Estates, Asheville, North Carolina

Boerner Botanical Garden, Hales Corner, Wisconsin

**Salt Lake Municipal Rose Garden**
1602 East 2100 South Sugarhouse
Salt Lake City 84106
801-467-0461
*1,330 plants, 170 varieties*
*AARS Garden*

---

VIRGINIA

**River Farm**
American Horticulture Society
7931 E. Boulevard Drive
Alexandria 22308
703-768-5700
*320 plants, 50 varieties*
*AARS Garden*

**Bon Air Memorial Rose Garden**
Bon Air Park
Wilson Boulevard and Lexington Street
Arlington 22152
703-644-4954
*3,500 plants, 125 varieties*
*AARS Garden*

**Confederate Cemetery**
Fourth and Taylor Street
Lynchburg 24506
*57 old garden roses*

**Norfolk Botanical Garden Bicentennial Rose Garden**
Norfolk 23518
804-441-5386
*4,000 plants, 213 varieties*
*AARS Garden*

**Woodlawn Plantation**
P.O. Box 37
Mount Vernon 22121
703-780-4000
*190 plants, 41 varieties*

**Fairhaven Rose Garden**
Fairhaven Park
Chuckanut Drive
Bellingham 98226
206-676-6801
*1,000 plants, 98 varieties*
*AARS Garden*

**Cornwall Park Rose Garden**
Cornwall Avenue
Bellingham 98550
*600 plants, 65 varieties*

**City of Chehalis Municipal Rose Garden**
80 Northeast Cascade Avenue
Chehalis 98532
206-748-0271
*290 plants, 50 varieties*
*AARS Garden*

**Bert Ross Memorial Rose Garden**
1611 Riverside Drive
Hoquiam 98227
*300 plants*

**Tri-Cities Rose Garden**
Lawrence Scott Memorial Park
Kennewick 99337
*200 plants*

**Carl S. English, Jr. Botanical Garden**
3015 Northwest 54th Street
Seattle 98107
206-783-7059
*250 plants, 4 varieties*

**Woodland Park Rose Garden**
5500 Phinney Avenue North
Seattle 98103
206-684-6880
*4,800 plants, 250 varieties*
*AARS Garden*

**Manito Gardens — Rose Hill**
4 West 21st Street
Spokane 99203
509-456-4331
*1,500 plants, 150 varieties*
*AARS Garden*

WEST VIRGINIA

**Ritter Park Rose Garden**
1500 McCoy Road
Huntington 25704
304-696-5543
*1,000 plants, 80 varieties*
*AARS Garden*

WISCONSIN

**Boerner Botanical Gardens**
5879 South 92nd Street
Hales Corners 55130
414-425-1130
*4,450 plants, 500 varieties*

**Longenecker Gardens of the University of Wisconsin Arboretum**
1207 Seminole Highway
Madison 53711
608-262-2746
*100 plants, 65 varieties*

**Oldbrich Botanical Garden**
3330 Atwood Avenue
Madison 53704
608-246-4551

**Paine Art Center and Arboretum**
1410 Algoma Boulevard
Oshkosh 54901
414-235-4530
*145 plants, 30 varieties*

CANADA

**Minter Gardens**
52892 Bunker Road
Rosedale British Columbia BOX 1X0
604-794-7191
*800 plants, 50 varieties*

**University of British Columbia Botanical Gardens**
601 N.W. Marine Drive
Vancouver, British Columbia V6T 1W5
604-228-2172
*350 varieties*

**Royal Botanical Gardens**
PO Box 399
Hamilton Ontario L8N 3H8
416-527-1158
*5,000 plants, 400 varieties*

**Niagara Parks Commission School of Horticulture**
PO Box 150
Niagara Falls Ontario L2N 6T2
416-354-8554
*2,800 plants, 60 varieties*

**Montreal Botanical Gardens**
4101 Sherwood Street East
Montreal H1X 2B2
514-872-1400
*8,000 plants, 215 varieties*

# Rose Organizations

**The American Rose Society**
P.O. Box 30,000
Shreveport, Louisiana 71130
Membership of over 20,000 primarily rose hobbyists, many of whom are interested in exhibiting rose shows. Publishes a soft-cover annual and *The American Rose,* a monthly magazine.

**The Canadian Rose Society**
Dianne D. Lask
686 Pharmacy Avenue
Scarsborough, Ontario
Canada MIL 3H8
Publishes a quarterly journal and an annual

**The Royal National Rose Society**
Chiswell Green
St. Albans, Hertfordshire
England AL2 3NR
Publishes a quarterly journal

Publishes quarterly *Heritage Roses Letter*

> North/East
> Miss Lily Shohan
> R.D. 1, Box 228
> Clinton Corners, NY 12514

> South/East
> Mr. Charles A. Walker
> 1512 Gorman Street
> Raleigh, NC 27606

North/Central
Dr. Henry Najat
6365 Wald Road
Monroe, WI 53566

South/Central
Ms. Mitzi VanSant
4806 Evans Avenue
Austin, TX 78751

North/West
Ms. Judi Dexter
23665 41st Avenue South
Kent, WA 98032

South/West: Initials A to L
Ms. Margaret Blodgett
1452 Curtis Street
Berkely, CA 94702

South/West: Initials M to Z
Ms. Frances Grate
472 Gibson Avenue
Pacific Grove, CA 93950

**Heritage Rose Foundation**
Mr. Charles A. Walker
1512 Gorman Street
Raleigh, North Carolina 27606

**Rose Hybridizers Association**
Mr. Larry D. Peterson
3245 Wheaton Road
Horseheads, NY 14845
Publishes quarterly newsletter

# Rose Publications

**Modern Roses 8:** This encyclopedic listing of rose varieties, published in 1980, is now out-of-print and somewhat out-of-date.
**Modern Roses 9** is a supplement to Modern Roses 8. Can be ordered from American Rose Society, P.O. Box 30,000, Shreveport, LA 71130

**Rosy Outlook,** quarterly magazine published by Carlyne (Rosy) J. McKenney, 1014 Enslen Avenue, Modesto, CA 95350

**The Yellow Rose,** publication of the Dallas Area Historical Rose Group, edited by Joe M. Woodard; 4216 Hockaday Drive, Dallas, TX 75229

**The Old Texas Rose,** newsletter of The Texas Rose Rustlers, quarterly. Ms. Margaret P. Sharpe, 9246 Kerrwood Lane, Houston 77080

**The Briar Patch** (formerly Sub-Rosa), quarterly newsletter of the Southern California Heritage Roses group, c/o Debbie and Roland Mettler, 3637 Empire Drive, Los Angeles, CA 90034

**Combined Rose List,** a yearly listing of all roses in commerce and cultivation, rose registrations update, hard-to-find roses and where to find them. Beverly R. Dobson, 215 Harriman Road, Irvington, NY 10533

**Beverly Dobson's Rose Letter** is a bi-monthly publication which includes features such as articles by recognized rose authorities, reviews of available rose literature, general rose news, interactive letters to the editor and insights into personalities of the rose world. It is available from Beverly R. Dobson, address above.

*Following pages:* The Cranford Rose Garden, Rose Day, 1990

# Glossary

**AARS:** All-America Rose Selections, Inc., an association of commercial rose growers dedicated to the testing and selection of new rose varieties.

**ARS:** The American Rose Society, a plant society devoted to the rose.

**Balling:** Occurs when the outer petals of a bloom adhere together and fail to open, usually due to damp weather conditions.

**Bedding plants:** Flowering plants suitable for planting together in beds. Most floribundas and many hybrid teas can be used this way.

**Bract:** A leaflike structure or pair of structures at the base of a flower or flowering shoot.

**Bristle:** A flexible, hairlike prickle. (See also *prickle*.)

**Bud:** Underdeveloped part of a shoot at the top of a stem or in an axil. Buds develop into shoots or flowers.

**Budded:** A rose plant that has grown from a bud of a desired variety grafted onto a suitable understock.

**Button-eye:** The effect in very double roses where the central petals curve inward, creating a small, round, buttonlike center. Seen in certain old garden roses.

**Calyx:** The outermost part of a flower, composed of five leafy, green sepals that protect the bud.

**Cane:** A rose stem. Canes have hard outer coverings and soft pithy centers.

**Climbers:** Rose varieties that have long canes and can clamber up convenient structures — or other plants — aided by their curved prickles.

**Deadheading:** Removing spent flowers to encourage reblooming.

**Double:** A rose bloom with many rows of petals.

**Exhibition Style, Exhibition Quality:** A rose bloom with long central petals that hold a high center as the outer petals unfurl in a symmetrical fashion. A rose that is one-third to three-quarters open is considered to be at exhibition stage. Varieties with fewer petals should be nearly one-third to one-half open, while varieties with many petals can be from one-half to three-quarters open.

**Grafted:** Condition where the desired variety of a rose is grafted onto a strong, vigorous rootstock. The form of grafting most commonly used for roses is bud-grafting, or budding.

**Heel In:** To store dormant, bare-root plants by completely burying them in the ground and keeping them moist until they can be planted in their permanent positions. Roses can be stored over winter in this manner.

**Hip:** The fleshy, cup-shaped structure around the base of a rose bloom containing the rose fruits.

**Hybrid:** A cross between two different species or varieties of roses.

**Hybrid Perpetual:** The popular garden rose from the mid-to-late 1800s, resulting from a number of chance crosses. Hybrid perpetuals are known as *remontant* roses, especially in Europe. This class of roses is a forerunner of the hybrid tea.

**Hybrid Tea:** The result of crossing tea roses with hybrid perpetuals. This class of roses is considered by many to be the ultimate development in rose breeding.

**Lateral:** Any rose cane that grows from a main cane. Smaller canes that grow from laterals are called sub-laterals.

**Node:** The point on a stem where a leaf and bud are found.

**Peduncle:** The stalk of a flower.

**Pegging:** The practice of securing the ends of flexible canes to the ground so that the shoots are held in a horizontal position. This produces a wider spread of bloom.

**Petal:** One of the units, usually showy, that make up the corolla of a flower. Petals surround the male parts (stamens) and the female parts (pistils) of a flower.

**Petiole:** Leaf stalk.

**Pillar Rose:** A rose variety, usually a short climber or rangy shrub, that has been trained to a post.

**Pistil:** The female part of a flower.

**Polyantha:** A dwarf rose, resulting from crossing the China with the *multiflora* roses. Polyanthas come into bloom late in the season and bloom continually until frost.

**Prickle:** The correct term for a rose "thorn." Roses do not have true thorns, which are modified branches; they have prickles, which may be stiff and hooked, flexible and straight (bristles), or glandular. Prickles arise from the outer layers of the stem and can easily be broken off.

**Procumbent:** Spreading; used to describe a rose with very lax canes. Roses with this type of growth habit are easily trained.

**Quartered:** Flowers whose central petals are formed into a number of segments. These are most commonly four sections, but three to five are also encountered. Quartering is seen especially among the old garden roses.

**Rambler:** A climbing rose with long, lax canes that can easily be trained to a fence or trellis. Ramblers come into bloom rather late in the season, and most bloom only once a season.

**Reflexed:** Term used to describe petals that curl back upon themselves. This often creates interesting patterns, such as star shapes, in the fully opened flower.

**Remontancy:** The ability to produce flowers after the main bloom.

**Rootstock, Understock:** The stronger, more vigorous rose variety on to which a bud is grafted. Varieties commonly used as understock are *R. multiflora*, 'Dr. Huey', and 'Fortuneana'.

**Semidouble:** Rose flowers with two rows of petals, or from seven to twenty-four petals. Such roses typically open up to show bright stamens in the center of the flower.

**Sepal:** One of the green leaf-like segments of the calyx. There are typically five sepals in a rose flower.

**Shrub rose:** Rose varieties that are difficult to classify have been put in a "shrub" category. Many newly developed varieties that cannot be classed as hybrid teas or floribundas are considered "modern shrub roses."

**Single:** A flower with five or ten petals in one or two whorls, five petals per whorl.

**Species Roses:** Roses that occur naturally in the wild. Species roses are not the result of man-made crossing.

**Sport:** An unusual branch formed by a genetic mutation in the growing bud. A sport often has flowers with a different appearance from the rest of the plant. Buds or cuttings from a sport will perpetuate the new characteristics.

**Stamen:** The male, pollen-producing, part of a flower.

**Standard Rose, Tree Rose:** A treelike form of a rose bush, the result of grafting a rose on to a sturdy cane either 2½ or 3½ feet from the ground. In some cases, the upright cane is itself the result of a vigorous variety having been budded on to a suitable rootstock. To assume symmetry, two or three buds may be grafted near the top of the standard. Standard roses require protection in severe weather conditions.

**Stipule:** One of a pair of leaflike outgrowths at the base of a leaf or petiole.

**Suckering:** Occurs when new shoots arise around the roots of a plant. This is undesirable in grafted plants because the sucker shoots come from the understock, not the budded, desirable rose. If all remain on the plant, the budded rose may eventually die because nutrients are directed into the sucker shoots.

**Thorns:** Roses do not have true thorns which are modified branches. (See *Prickle*.)

**Tissue-Cultured Rose:** A rose grown in a sterile culture medium in the laboratory from the tissue of a parent plant. A tissue-cultured rose is an exact duplication of its parent.

**Understock:** See *Rootstock*.

**Very Double:** Rose blooms with a great many petals are called "very double." Often they are quartered and have a "button-eye." Some very double roses occur in the old garden rose group. Centifolias, for example, may have more petals than the hundred their name suggests.

# Bibliography

**Adams, Charles G.** "Rosifying American Highways."
*The American Rose Annual* (1921), 44–46.

**Allen, R. C., Robert Pyle, Louis M. Massey, and
Arthur F. Truex.** "John Horace McFarland, L.H.D."
*The American Rose Annual* (1949), 3–12.

**Beales, Peter.** *Classic Roses.* New York: Holt,
Rinehart and Winston, 1985.

**Bean, W. J.** *Trees and Shrubs Hardy in the British
Isles.* Volume IV. Eighth Edition Revised, 1980.
Reprinted with Corrections, 1981. Reprint.
London: John Murray, 1989.

*Bev Dobson's Rose Letter.* Irvington, N.Y.: Beverly R.
Dobson, 1983–.

**Buist, Robert.** *The Rose Manual.* 1844. Facsimile
reprint. New York: Coleman, 1978.

**Caparn, Harold A.** "A Rose-Garden with a Reason."
*The American Rose Annual* (1918), 24–28.

———. "About Municipal Rose-Gardens."
*The American Rose Annual* (1925), 35–42.

———. "Designing a Small Rose-Garden."
*The American Rose Annual* (1925), 43–49.

———. "Roses in the Landscape."
*The American Rose Annual* (1939), 129–31.

———. "Making a Municipal Rose-Garden."
*The American Rose Annual* (1941), 59–60.

———. "What Rose Bushes to Use, and Where."
*The American Rose Annual* (1941), 49–53.

———. "The Brooklyn Rose-Garden."
*The American Rose Annual* (1942), 112–14.

**Corbett, L. C.** "Continuing Dr. Van Fleet's Work."
*The American Rose Annual* (1924), 27–28.

**Crockett, James U.** *Roses.* Time-Life Encyclopedia
of Gardening. Revised edition. Alexandria, Va.:
Time-Life Books, 1978.

**Dawson, Charles A.** "The Roses in Colonial Virginia."
*The American Rose Annual* (1949), 31–37.

**Dobson, Beverly R.** *Combined Rose List.*
Irvington, N.Y.: Beverly R. Dobson, 1989.

"Dr. Walter Van Fleet, American Rosarian and Plant
Hybridist: An Appreciation by Some of his Friends
and Associates." *The American Rose Annual*
(1922), 13–22.

**Ellwanger, H. B.** *The Rose.* Revised edition.
New York: Dodd, Mead & Co., 1923.

**Fisher, John.** *The Companion to Roses.* Topsfield, Mass.:
Salem House, 1987.

**Free, Montague.** *The Rose Garden of the Brooklyn
Botanic Garden.* Brooklyn Botanic Garden Record,
vol. XXVIII, no. 3. Brooklyn, N.Y.: The Brooklyn
Institute of Arts and Sciences, 1939.

**Harkness, Jack.** *Roses and how to grow them.* London: Dent, 1978.

———. *The World's Favorite Roses.* New York:
McGraw-Hill, 1979.

**McFarland, J. Horace.** "Great Public Rose-Gardens."
*The American Rose Annual* (1918), 36–40.

———. "New Uses of Climbing Roses." *The American Rose
Annual* (1918), 86–89.

———. *The Rose in America.* NY: Mcmillan, 1923.

———. "Seventy-Five Years with Roses." *The American Rose
Annual* (1946), 3–8.

———. *Memoirs of a Rose Man.* Emmaus, Penn.: Rodale, 1949.

*Modern Roses 8: The International Check-list of Roses.* Edited
by C. E. Meikle. Harrisburg, Pa.: McFarland, 1980.

*Modern Roses 9: The International Checklist of Roses.* Edited by
P. A. Haring, Shreveport, La.: The American
Rose Society, 1986.

**Morrison, B. Y.** "Carrying on Dr. Van Fleet's Work." *The
American Rose Annual* (1926). 41–46.

**Morrison, Ernest.** "Dr. Rose." *Apprise* (June 1989), 40–47.

"Municipal Rose-Gardens in 1939: An Editorial Survey."
*The American Rose Annual* (1939), 133–50.

Parker, G. A. "The Rose-Garden in Elizabeth Park, Hartford, Conn." *The American Rose Annual* (1916), 69–72.

Parsons, S. B. *The Rose*. New York: Wiley & Halsted, 1856.

Paul, William. *The Rose Garden*. 1848. Facsimile reprint. New York: Coleman, 1978.

Phillips, Roger, and Martyn Rix. *Roses*. New York: Random House, 1988.

Prince, William Robert. *Prince's Manual of Roses*. 1846. Facsimile reprint. New York: Coleman, 1979.

Pyle, Robert. "The Distribution of Some New Van Fleet Roses." *The American Rose Annual* (1921), 32–34.

Rockwell, F. F., and Esther C. Grayson. *The Rockwells' Complete Book of Roses*. New York: Doubleday, 1958.

*Roses*. The Time-Life Gardener's Guide. Alexandria, Va.: Time-Life Books, 1989.

Shepherd, Roy E. *History of the Rose*. 1954. Facsimile reprint. New York: Coleman, 1978.

*Taylor's Guide to Roses*. Boston: Houghton Mifflin, 1986.

Thomas, George C., Jr. *The Practical Book of Outdoor Rose Growing*. Philadelphia and London: Lippincott, 1917.

"Two New Van Fleet Roses." *The American Rose Annual* (1926), 47–49.

Van Fleet, W. "Possibilities in the Production of American Garden Roses." *The American Rose Annual* (1916), 27–36.

———. "On the 1916 Rose Firing-Line." *The American Rose Annual* (1917), 41–43.

———. "Notes from the Rose Firing-Line." *The American Rose Annual* (1918), 43–45.

———. "Fragrant Roses." *The American Rose Annual* (1919), 14–20.

———. "Rose-Breeding Notes for 1918." *The American Rose Annual* (1919), 29–34.

———. "Rose-Breeding Notes for 1919." *The American Rose Annual* (1920), 23–30.

———. "Rose-Breeding in 1920 at Bell Experiment Plot." *The American Rose Annual* (1921), 25–31.

Watson, David B. "The Medical Properties of the Rose." *The American Rose Annual* (1944), 29–33.

White, Edward A. **"The Progress of the Rose in America."** *Gardeners' Chronicle of America*, (March 1922), 26:80–82.

Wilson, E. H. "What Roses Does America Need?" *The American Rose Annual* (1924), 23–25.

Wright, Richardson. "Pages in American Rose History." *Gardeners' Chronicle* (July 1939), 43:202–203, 230.

Wyman, Donald. "Again, Rose Species." *The American Rose Annual* (1941), 46–48.

Young, Norman. *The Complete Rosarian*. Edited by L. H. Wyatt. New York: St. Martin's Press, 1971.

# Index

# Index of Roses

**(bold face = photogaph)**